Zombie L♥ve

The Do's, Don'ts, and It Depends of Undead Dating

Jeff Busch, Ph.Z

STERLING
New York

STERLING
New York

An Imprint of Sterling Publishing
387 Park Avenue South
New York, NY 10016

ISBN 978-1-4027-9228-1 (paperback)
ISBN 978-1-4027-9229-8 (ebook)

Library of Congress Cataloging-in-Publication Data

Busch, Jeffrey, 1962–
    Zombie love : the do's, don'ts, and it depends of undead dating / by Jeff Busch, Ph.Z.
    p. cm.
ISBN 978-1-4027-9228-1 (print book) — ISBN 978-1-4027-9229-8 (ebook)
1. Zombies—Humor. 2. Dating (Social customs)—Humor. I. Title.
PN6231.Z65B87 2012
818'.602—dc23

2011038780

Distributed in Canada by Sterling Publishing
c/o Canadian Manda Group, 165 Dufferin Street
Toronto, Ontario, Canada M6K 3H6
Distributed in the United Kingdom by GMC Distribution Services
Castle Place, 166 High Street, Lewes, East Sussex, England BN7 1XU
Distributed in Australia by Capricorn Link (Australia) Pty. Ltd.
P.O. Box 704, Windsor, NSW 2756, Australia

For information about custom editions, special sales, and premium and
corporate purchases, please contact Sterling Special Sales at 800-805-5489
or specialsales@sterlingpublishing.com.

Manufactured in the United States of America

2   4   6   8   10   9   7   5   3   1

www.sterlingpublishing.com

CONTENTS

INTRODUCTION

Dating isn't always easy. In fact, it can be downright terrifying. You would think since your heart stopped beating it would be easier to let someone into your chest cavity, but opening up is just as scary for the undead as it is for the living. All of the insecurities you had when alive probably followed you to the grave and rose back up stronger than ever, just like you.

But don't despair. Even though you're a foul, rotting, reanimated corpse driven by a hunger for living flesh, finding romance is not impossible. Some of the challenges remain the same, like where do you go to find a date? Some will be new, like what if he/she/it is repulsed by your exposed muscle tissue?

YOUR AFTERLIFE GUARD

Zombie Love is here to help you navigate the waters of the befouled dating pool and hunt down your better half. You will learn how to make informed decisions by asking yourself eternally applicable questions: Who or what is your ideal lover? What does it mean to slip on that ring? And does that particular individual still have a finger on which to actually wear that ring?

There are quizzes along the way that will steer your romantic aspirations in the attainable (not edible) direction. Look, it's not brain surgery to find a brainless beauty; you just need to nail down what it is you're looking for. And then you will know just where to find it—be it at the communal dinner spot in the woods or at a singles zombie shamble. This book is packed with more ideas than you can shake a bat at on where and how to get a date.

YOUR PERSON(ISH)AL TRAINER

Once you land a dead one, *Zombie Love* will teach you the art of planning the perfect date. Just because your flesh is mostly rotten doesn't mean running a comb through your hair and covering up your stank with some odor neutralizers doesn't help. Looks (and smells) still count! With *Zombie Love* in your back pocket, you can get over those nerves you thought died when you did. Just relax, take a deep ragged breath, and remember that the zombie sitting across the torch-lit table from you is experiencing the same sensation of maggots in their stomach that you are.

But what if you're sitting across from a hot fleshbag—one that elicits a different kind of hunger? *Zombie Love* has the answers on breaking the taboo of inter-living dating, dealing with the prejudice against it, and resisting love at first bite.

YOUR POST-LIFE COACH

After you've mastered the first date, you're bound to get a second one, and before you know it, you're in a relationship! The view on love is a little different with a post-death perspective. Be prepared for a whole new breed of issues. For example, having dinner with a significant other's family is always awkward, but it'll be a nightmare if you treat Aunt Gladys like an appetizer.

If you have gotten past all of those stages, you might be hearing wedding bells (if your ears haven't sloughed off yet, of course). Tying the knot means more than deciding between post-modern furniture or the comfort of moldering rags and a cool dirt pit. And you can trust this book to help you discern what battles are worth fighting and when you should just groan and make up.

Through all the trials and tribulations of dating and beyond when beyond the grave, *Zombie Love* will be your unfaltering guide to reanimating the ragged wad of muscle that used to be your heart. After all, nobody wants to end up alone the second time around.

FORAGING FOR LOVE

DIGGING AROUND IN THE RIGHT PLACES

Whether you're a not-so-fresh-faced teenager wading into the contaminated waters of the undead dating pool for the first time or a well-preserved veteran slowly creaking back into the saddle, dating can be an intimidating experience.

WHERE DO YOU EVEN START?

For the newcomers, the world of attractive flesheaters seems like it's shrouded in mystery. You ask yourself, *How do I approach someone I like? What do I say?* Do you simply shamble up to someone you find attractive and ask them out, or do you get to know them before asking for a proper date? Would they prefer to go for fast food pulled into the shadows of a back alley or a fancy meal that's been thoughtfully laid out on the cement floor of a trash-strewn warehouse?

The answers depend on both who you are and how you think that zombie may respond. Consider both your character and theirs from the get-go. If you are a gregarious night stalker who is great at initiating interesting conversations, then by all means dazzle your prey! If you're more of a reserved revenant, then you need an arsenal of icebreakers to get the conversation going. Either way—unless you've been professionally embalmed—time is not on your side, so get to it!

PROTECT YOURSELF AND WHAT USED TO BE YOUR HEART

When it comes to matters of your heart, err on the side of caution. Sure, unlife seems smooth and slow-moving in movies like *Night of the Living Dead*, but the real world is a little more barbed. Even though your heart is no longer beating, it can still be broken by zombies and breathers alike. There is an intense bias against the life-challenged, so be mindful on the dating scene. Chatting up a bonny lifer may be met with a friendly smile, but you're more likely to get a shrill scream followed by a thwack to the head.

NEW TO THE DATING SCENE?

So, you just recovered from your post-life/pre-reanimated slumber and cleared the fog from your eyes (or blood, depending on your circumstances). Now, take a good, long look at yourself in the mirror.

HEY, GOOD LOOKING!

You may notice things are a little different than they used to be, but remember that this is a whole new life (sort of), and the standards of beauty have changed. If you died with minimal trauma, your complexion might be in good shape and all you need is a little rouge, cover-up, and a quick comb through your hair to keep the whimpering of passersby to a minimum. Throw on a pair of sunglasses and a new shirt and you might just pass for a lifer! Consider yourself lucky; very few of the undead start off in such good condition.

If you are part of the majority who begin their post-death existence with some visible damage, rest easy in the fact that you are not alone. You may not be attractive in the traditional sense, but you can be a hottie by the new zombie standards—a rottie!

DEALING WITH DECAY

Just like in life, your looks can fade. Be sure to maintain yourself and pay attention to any new leaks or bullet holes. Be it a minor scratch from another undead or a vicious bite from a duel over scraps with a pit bull, these damages need to be tended to immediately. A little duct tape can go a long way! (More on page 54.) Ask the gal at your local department store makeup counter for some tips and consider taking an auto body repair course. Staying on top of your decay is crucial for maintaining your sex appeal.

You'll soon notice that your joints are tighter than they used to be. Don't be too concerned when you hear cracking and popping and an occasional tearing. These are just the weaker connective tissues failing and gas bubbles escaping from various places that were once tight with rigor mortis but are now loosened by decomposition—it's totally normal. By concentrating on your balance (a tumble could result in crucial limb loss) you'll achieve the stiffened, lumbering gait all undead know and love.

THE NEW YOU!

Once you're comfortable in your new skin and are moving with appropriate awkwardness, you'll start to notice some other good things. For instance, you don't tire as much as before, and you're unremittingly driven by a new-found hunger for fresh flesh. Food has never tasted better, and the workout you need to catch it will keep off those extra pounds! In fact, you'll find it difficult to maintain your pre-death weight without daily meals. Ingest at minimum a toddler's worth of protein everyday to keep up that masculine physique or girlish figure—something that can be especially difficult to come by if you live in a well-armed neighborhood or Texas.

You'll also quickly see that things don't hurt the way they used to. A finger caught in a slammed steel door may not be noticed until you see the sad little nubbin where it used to be. And a shotgun to the midsection won't slow you down as you chomp down on Grandma at the family picnic. Good times, great body!

UNLIFE IS GOOD

In addition to your pain-free existence, you should notice enhanced senses of smell and taste (and maybe a few other enhanced senses, if you know what I mean). Your speed and agility have been replaced with a dogged determination and relentless, burning hunger. So go out there and unlive a little!

Now that you know the new afterlife you a little better, it's time to focus on matters of the heart. Not the delicious, still-beating, belly-filling ones but the kind that dictates happiness and make an emotionally fulfilling post-death existence possible. Seriously, who said romance is dead?

THINGS MAY HAVE CHANGED SINCE YOU LEFT THE DATING SCENE

How long has it been since you last dated? If you were married or in a monogamous relationship for an extended period of time, you will find that things have changed indeed. The rules may seem a lot looser. Many of the undead, perhaps you included, have an a newfound desire to roam the land, looking for new experiences. Even if you were a serial dater, finding that groove may not be as easy as it once was. Zombies may often travel in hordes, making your options plentiful, but it can be hard to break the ice with a well-timed witticism over the groans, screams, and shotgun blasts—the regular soundtrack that accompanies most shambling gangs of undead. The truth is, reentering the dating pool at any depth is tough, regardless of your stage of decomposition.

A DEEPER/DARKER WORLD

Societal rules are a little different now. Consider dining with your lady: One lass may think it a gallant gesture for you to hold open a skull for her to nibble, while another may be totally offended due to her modern sense of independence. What a state!

If you are a man, you are still expected to bring a token of affection on a first date. A bouquet of daisies might be sweet (albeit a little Frankensteiny), whereas a baggie of chocolate-filled filter organs might delight her to pieces.

If you're a woman, think about what you expect. Do you let him pay or do you go dutch? A lady of a latter era may expect him to unzip her body bag whereas a modish gal may find that completely ghastly. What kind of afterlifer are you?

HOW TO COPE

Social mores change regularly, so do a little research on what's trending since you reanimated. Men, grab a couple copies of the most popular gal rags (*Pallor, Cadaver Monthly*) for tips and inroads to what the ladies are wearing, watching, and doing. Women, be sure to read some of the top dude glossies (*GCorpse*, *8-Cylinder*, etc.) for current rages in men's attire, hobbies, and humor.

Acceptable topics of discussion have also changed over the years. In the past, it was considered uncouth to discuss politics, religion, or degrees of decomposition in mixed or unfamiliar company. Today, almost any topic is considered fair game on a date, especially if you truly wish to get to know someone's sensibilities. Though this kind of talk can spark some fiery debate, so you may want to avoid it on a first date.

Depending on what decade you became a member of the undead, this evolution of social mores can be perceived as progress or a huge aberration. You'll have to accept them and adapt, or crawl back into your worm-infested hole and settle for spending your afterlife alone.

THE BRIGHT SIDE

These are truly exciting times to be on the reanimated dating scene! Don't be intimidated. With so many new opportunities at your bony fingertips, it's much easier to find that special something. There are countless digital outlets, ranging from online dating services to special-interest chat rooms that make the furry community look tame by comparison. These groups even go offline and gather in church basements, community centers, and fence-free cemeteries to connect and share a snack.

With all these new tools and understanding at your disposal, you'll never be alone! Even those who are the most ravaged by decomposition or small-arms fire can now find another who's suffered the same—or a little worse off—and is willing to overlook a little bit of pus and gangrene.

ZOMBIE LOVE

THE DIFFERENCE BETWEEN LIVING-ON-LIVING AND ZOMBIE-ON-ZOMBIE DATING

Your pre-reanimated dating routine was something you did without thought. Perhaps a long, relaxing prep shower followed by a thorough personal grooming ritual and then picking out a sexy look for the night. You would take a last-minute glance in the mirror to check your tie or apply that last swipe of mascara, do a final breath check, and off you'd go. Pretty standard stuff.

THE WAY WE WERE
You'd meet him or her at the chicest dinner spot, throw back a few long-stemmed bubblies, and engage in a blissful (often vapid) conversation popping with giggles and coy smiles. If all was going well, maybe you'd follow up with a movie or a jaunt to the hottest club in town for some more drinks and maybe a little boogie on the dance floor.

At the end of the date you'd part ways (or not, if you've got a lot of good moves and libations), excited about the night's revelries and optimistically looking forward to the next date. Yes, your pre-zombie existence was pretty good in retrospect.

THE WAY IT IS
Things now are a wee bit more difficult. For starters, your prep time has most likely tripled. That leisurely shower has been replaced with body inspections for loosening and lost tissue in need of repair or removal. Once you've reinforced your structural integrity, you should probably color correct those problem areas with liberal amounts of makeup. "Putting on your face" is going to take on a whole new meaning for you.

Finding the right outfit can be a dead-leg drag. Since the leaking body fluids or garbage stains inflicted by an angry mini-mob can happen at any moment, you should stick to dark colors and make friends with stain guard sprays. Nonetheless, you will have to replace your wardrobe often, so don't break the bank on a single shopping trip. Stock up on discount clothing at wholesale or consignment stores.

GETTING THERE IS HALF THE PROBLEM

Your car probably went to a fleshbag sibling during your stint underground, and public transportation is not exactly undead-friendly. So before you have your sweetie by your side, find out which bus, train, or cab service has easy-to-clean vinyl seating and a progressive attitude.

Now where do you two lovecrows go? Look for a restaurant or bar that is more accepting of your kind and serves satisfying cuisine. Calling ahead to talk to the maître d' works, or just lurk outside a place to see if it has a stench-ridden, romantic aura.

IT'S NOT ALL BAD!

In fact, some of it is better. You may have to worry about cosmetics and simple-minded breathers, but as a zombie you must learn that these problems are superficial. Get beneath that which is skin-deep, and you will find the juicy, delicious meat of the afterlife.

For instance, you will notice your primal hunger for brains is matched only by your carnal hunger for pleasure. Long gone are the days of inhibitions—now is the time of unbridled passion! You will likely be unable to control your desires for long, because the whole zombie deal is wild, irrepressible need. The best part? Your date will be like-minded! Once you discover that you share the same physical problems and proclivities, you will experience a freedom your human mind wouldn't have dared dream of.

WHAT ARE YOUR PRIORITIES?

You may be a rotting corpus with a desire for flesh, but you still have needs. What are you looking for in that something that will make you feel whole (even if you are a little holey)? Important qualities to flirt with are: sharing a sense of humor and parallel interests; professional embalmment; and, of course, looks as well as rate and stage of decomposition. Just because you're both reanimated corpses doesn't mean looks don't figure into the equation.

You'll likely have to make some concessions from your pre-zombie standards, but if you take the time to care for yourself, you'll want a partner who does the same. Perhaps you're looking for someone in an earlier stage of decay—a lot of zombies prefer a little meat on the bone.

And don't forget values—the biggie being religion. If you keep kosher, can you date someone who chows down on saucy Mennonites? Or what if they only nibble on patchouli-steeped vegans while you favor the double-meat goodness of a carni-vore? Depending on how staunchly you hold onto your values, differences like these may lead to a lot of arguing over the dinner pit.

WHAT CAN'T YOU NOT LIVE WITHOUT?

Amenities you thought as must-haves in life may have lost their luster in your afterlife. Landing the latest hot ride or the one hundredth generation iPhone probably doesn't seem nearly as important as the need to home in on a lone city worker at dawn—though if there's an app for that, you may still want to upgrade your smartphone.

Yesterday you were a fashionista, painfully aware that he was wearing last season's loafers, or you were a plastic surgeon who plumped up your wife's lips and tits to make her smokin'.

Are you still that "person" now that you call a shallow ditch in the forest home? You may have a few physical zombie preferences (blonde, brunette, or skinless), but other material matters have probably fallen to the wayside. A deal breaker today could simply be that your lover ate that old plastic surgeon husband before reattaching a missing limb.

Take some time to really delve deep and think about what you can nonlive with and what you can't nonlive without.

GIVE CHANGE A CHANCE
Just face it—change is a part of both life and unlife. Needs and desires always have and always will ebb and flow. When you were alive, your opinions and requirements evolved with age and experience. Youth catered to that cute someone who had a car; the twenties heralded a fella or a gal who had planned out their future; and with maturity came the want for a responsible mate with a mortgage and a dream of a bouncing baby or four.

Now, as a member of the living impaired, your priorities will continue to develop with the different stages in your nonlife. At first you may yearn for a reanimate who has experience under its belt to show you the ropes of your new existence. Then you may find yourself longing for deeper meaning and a cuddle under the moonlight or delivery dock.

CHECK IN WITH YOURSELF
Because your rotting skin isn't the only thing about you that's continually changing, it's a good idea to reevaluate where your head and heart stand every once in a while. You may find it challenging to sort through all your feelings simply in your mind. With a slowly deteriorating brain, thoughts can easily become scrambled, so it helps to make a list. Things get a lot clearer when you put them down on paper.

To get you started, grab a bloody nib and try the quiz on pages 21–22. It is psychologically designed to evaluate the needs and desires of the undead heart. Going deeper than the common lust for brains and love of terror in small children's eyes, it will help you determine the qualities you need in a lasting partner.

WHAT A ZOMBIE WANTS, WHAT A ZOMBIE NEEDS

It's time to dig deep to figure out what you are looking for in an expired life partner. Read each question carefully and write down your answer on a separate piece of paper. To unearth your true undead needs, answer as honestly as possible. The result will be a less gloomy idea of what you're looking for. Then you can focus when out on the prowl, avoid the corpses that are all wrong for you and dig up the one that's just ripe.

MIND AND SOUL (SORT OF)

1. What do you value most: honesty, faithfulness, or an agile mind that out-thinks capture?

2. Is a sense of humor meaningful?

3. Is it important that one respects their elders?

4. Is it important that one does not eat their elders?

5. Which is more important: intelligence or brains?

6. How about limbs or intestines?

7. Skin or skinned?

8. Screw, marry, and eat—who would you pick for each? George W. Bush, Johnny Depp, and Robert Pattinson; or Hillary Clinton, Tina Fey, and Katy Perry.

9. Do you prefer something that devours a sweaty club-hopper or a dapper museum patron?

10. Do you prefer a cat- or dog-lover?

11. Do you prefer a cat- or dog-eater, or strictly human?

12. Do you get along with something that has stalwart opinions on zombie rights or that is happy just to follow the crowd and pick off the stragglers?

13. Is kindness a weakness or a virtue?

14. An open mind: Is it a flaw or a strength?

15. Is an open wound a sign of weakness or a turn-on?

BODY AND BRAWN

1. How important is someone's physical appearance?

2. Given the fact that you're a reanimated corpse, are you really one to judge?

3. Do you like tall drinks of water or petite packages?

4. What is your favorite eye color?

5. If the eyes are missing, can you still lose yourself in the limpid pools of hollowed-out sockets?

6. Is connecting on an emotional level enough if someone is missing a limb or an erogenous zone?

7. Is there a body part you can't unlive without?

8. Are you okay with the ever-present stench of decay, or is formaldehyde a must?

9. Do you prefer Kirstie Alley from her days on *Cheers* or *Fat Actress*? Alternatively, Alec Baldwin in *The Hunt for Red October* or *30 Rock*?

10. How much Bondo is too much Bondo?

11. Are you attracted to any specific nationality?

12. Because Asian chicks are really hot, am I right?

13. Do you think true beauty really lies on the inside?

14. Do you prefer the smell of naturally-occurring bodily odors or lemon-scented industrial disinfectants?

15. Do you like big butts? Are you unable to lie?

BAD DATE TERRITORY

The test you just took is only meant as a general compass to help you find your brain-eating sweetie. But once you put your love-finding to the challenge, you may stumble into a crazy or two, a leech, or an overzealous creeper. Here are a few personality profiles to date with caution, or, better yet, avoid.

BEWARE MOST BREATHERS

Zombies are from Pluto, and the living are from Venus. *Zombie Love* will explore this taboo a little later, but let's get the most disastrous issues out of the way.

Type one: the bigots. These people have an exaggerated fear of resurrection, and they show their feelings with manic pride on their bumpers: "Honk if you shot a zombie today." Dating this kind of fleshsack is slim, but beware—a romantic moonlit movie might turn into a trap for some target practice.

Type two: the experimenter. These dilettantes have no real sense of commitment and are only looking to take a break from a warm body. They are fickle and will drop you faster than some dirty gauze. So even though being with them is comforting because they remind you of your living days and you know they won't try to immolate you, they will likely hurt you in other ways. You may be undead, but that doesn't mean you can't suffer from a broken heart.

SOMETHING OLD, SOMETHING NEW, BOTH WILL MAKE YOU BLUE

The newly undead are not looking for a solid relationship. You remember that feeling: All you wanted to do was find someone to pal around with and maybe share a bone over, but the ever-after was never in the plans. They'll start out clingy then quickly change gears to flighty. Keep them around as a pal, but don't get too attached.

AVOID THE DECREPIT

Those who don't take care of themselves and have really pro-
gressed in their deterioration are to be avoided as well. Good
zombie hygiene is the mark of a happy zombie. If you spot
excessive deterioration, walk away. These things are only minutes
away from the second grave and are apt to turn into a puddle of
putrescent goo on a hot day. Who needs that kind of brain drain?

BEWARE THE STALKER AND THE GREEN-EYED MONSTER

Repeated phone calls from a heavy breather. Being shadowed
down a lonely alley. Sound like a horror movie? Try again—it's
that clingy reanimate that inflicts a level of soulsucking attachment
worse than death. They need to be hosed down with constant
attention to feel good about themselves, and who has the energy
to prop someone up like that? Shuffle away from this one as fast
as your stiff stagger can.

Jealousy can be a particularly dangerous emotion in reanimates. A little bit can be flattering, but an undead green-eyed
monster that devours your friends and coworkers because it
"didn't like the way she looked at you" is not someone you want
to keep around. If you sense a jealous streak in your partner,
figure out fast how wide it is. If you're deleting a lot of contacts
from your phone for reasons of decapitation, you better shamble
away as fast as you can.

NO NEED FOR THE NEEDY

Oh woe, this group will drain you like a vampire on a supple
neck…not to mention they will put a big dent in your supply of
duct tape and silicone adhesives. Do you really want someone
calling you at 2AM to reattach a digit lost to a stronger-than-
she-looked preschooler? You've made it this far as a survivor,
and you deserve someone who is just as able-bodied as you
to escape from a hairy situation on its own. You sure as hell
don't want your ass filled with buckshot just because of a whiny
weakling who can't hack post-death on its own two legs.

MEETING THAT SPECIAL SOMETHING

While it may seem too easy, your regular haunts really do work. You go to a place where you can explore your interests in things like books, music, and throbbing flesh. And you know what you'll find there? A like-minded zombie. So keep your eyes peeled everywhere you normally go—from the mundane grocery store to your favorite watering hole—and lurking in the shadows is sure to be a mate who shares your tastes (and wants to share something tasty if you're lucky).

CLUBS AND RESTAURANTS

Those trendy bars and clubs you patronized as a mortal can be just as appealing to your undead sensibilities when you loiter in their back alleys. Not only may you find a tasty couple of club-goers swapping bodily fluids while "getting some fresh air," you might bump into a flesheating hottie bouncing to the bass beat on the same mission as you. You can then compliment them on their hunting skills and strike up a conversation as you snack on what used to be pretty young things.

THE PARK

The next time you need to stretch those atrophying legs, consider doing it on a foggy, moonless evening. You're just asking for a moviemaking moment. But if you choose a sunny day, your bravery can be rewarded when you lock eyes with a revenant who doesn't notice your blemishes or ax wounds. This is the one who can stomach every kind of wound, goo, or issues of the heart you come across, and if you find the gaping shotgun blast in their chest oddly alluring, then you may have found a match that will last!

PLACES OF WORSHIP

Traditional religions don't exactly look favorably on the newly risen (unless your name starts with a "J" and you're only around for three days). But faith didn't die with you. In fact it can be renewed at your local temple or church. Crouch behind an altar and you may find a companion with a similar sacrilegious taste for the warm, still-beating hearts of congregants. Then chow down on the bodies and drink the blood of the devout while engaging in a conversation about the irony of it all.

STORES AND MALLS

Dawn of the Dead was never more right—zombies love shopping (and attacking en masse)! Many have found their true loves while simply shopping for everyday items. You see a pretty brunette with shears between her shoulder blades shopping for sandwich bags? While avoiding the mall cops, lend her some advice on how to prevent freezer burn to your sweetbreads. She might reward your kindness with an invite to eat leftovers together.

A recently reanimated young man is easily confused by the myriad variety of cover-up shades in the cosmetics aisle. He knows a flayed and moldy jaw can be a tad off-putting, so he'll really appreciate any advice offered by a flirtatious flesheater. If the conversation goes well, offer to help apply it the first time—at your hideout.

FESTIVALS AND OUTDOOR EVENTS

Street fairs and block parties are great for mingling among the living without sending them screaming. Everyone's in a booze haze or has sunstroke, so you're all in the same lumbering state. The ball pit is like bobbing-for-apples for the undead, attracting a feeding frenzy of eminently dateable rotties. You can check out the haunted house for a veritable conveyor-belt buffet. Breathers will think you're just part of the ride, so you can pick off the plumpest snacks while scoping out a prospective valentine who shares your passion for all things ghoulish.

100 ZOMBIE COUPLES AND WHERE THEY MET

The proof is in the percentages, so try out these zombie meeting hot spots to find a proper inamorata.

40% Stumbling about in Grand Guignol fashion, covered in gore and silhouetted against a bloodred full moon.

14% In alleys outside clubs while stalking partygoers who had stepped out for a quick smoke.

12% In sandboxes behind day care centers.

10.5% During Spring Outbreak 2011 at Daytona Beach.

9% On blind dates set up by friends who insisted they each had wonderful personalities, were good with children, pets, and old people, and couldn't figure out why prizes like them hadn't been snatched up years ago, for goodness' sake.

4% While eyeing the butcher at the supermarket.

3.5% While simultaneously discovering the remains of hobos hit by freight trains.

3% At a zombie crawl (one couple met while being awarded for their "costumes" before devouring the celebrity judge).

2% While emerging from fresh graves.

1.75% At a major sporting event.

.25% At a bris.

(Percentage of a fraction indicates this was the primary initial location.)

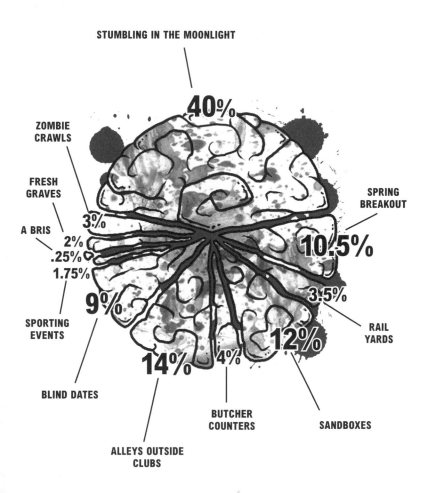

STUMBLING IN THE MOONLIGHT

40%

ZOMBIE
CRAWLS

FRESH
GRAVES

SPRING
BREAKOUT

A BRIS

3%

2%

.25%

1.75%

10.5%

9%

3.5%

SPORTING
EVENTS

RAIL
YARDS

14%

4%

12%

BLIND DATES

BUTCHER
COUNTERS

SANDBOXES

ALLEYS OUTSIDE
CLUBS

HAVE YOUR FRIENDS SET YOU UP

Sometimes your family, coworkers, and hunting buddies know you better than you know yourself. That makes them great matchmakers for you, finding parallels between your weaknesses (kittens in a basket) and a single undead's strengths (breaking down walls to devour the kittens' owner).

WHY THIS WORKS

These lifers and life-challenged not only knew you as a kid, they saw you through your funeral and now in the unlife. They get your gallows humor and have lent a bony shoulder to leak your ocular cavities on for Undead Independence Day.

They know your tastes and have your best interest at heart; they can potentially set you up with something great! You may be hesitant at first to accept a set up. Blind dates can be awkward. What if you show up and he/she/it is disgusting, more so than you are? What does that say about how your friends see you? But chances are if they like you, they like another zombie similar to you that is of the opposite sex (or not—whatever floats your boat across the Acheron), and a friend set up could really work out in your favor.

AND IF IT DOESN'T

If it turns out that you and your blind date get along like rotting flesh and the sun, do not let this come between you and the friend who made the introduction. They meant well, so don't go ripping their heads off because your date wasn't up to snuff. Also try not to rip your date's head off, as your mutual friend will not appreciate that either. Be polite and sensitive when letting them know that things just didn't work out. Plus, you don't want to ruin your chances of your pal setting you up with their hot, newly dead sibling. Aoooga!

SINGLES SHAMBLES AND MEAT-AND-GREETS

You may not have been one to boogie or pick up a paintbrush before, but learning the Monster Mash or Z-ball may be your gateway to a new hobby and honey.

SINGLE AND READY TO MANGLE

Remember when you used to go to the student center to pick up chicks (or dudes) by telling them you worked at the college radio station? Well, it always worked, right? That's because *doing* something made you look hot.

It's no different now. No one likes a deadbeat undead without any interest in activities and diversions. Break the boredom and enroll in a zombie-centric singles event. The living have their uncorking parties and furries conventions, and we have our own meat-and-greets that are perfect for finding a like-minded spirit.

HARPY HOUR AND TASTING NIGHTS

Meeting across a coagulating mug of muck can be done casually at a bar or at a more civilized venue during an organized affair. Singles shambles, harpy hours, and co-dead sports leagues are all relatively new—and incredibly fruitful—ways to find that special someone or something. If faith is an important part of your afterlife, you may want to try events sponsored by religious groups like Rejewvenates for Jesus or Voodooism.

Fluid-and-flesh pairing events are good for the more sophisticated revenant. The best ones are held in graveyards shortly after a new burial. To find some in your area, ask around in the alley behind your local wine store or gourmet delicatessen.

PHYSICAL ACTIVITIES

Dances/shuffles and organized sports leagues are marvelous if you can manage more than a slow straggle and still have most of your limbs. Be cautious, though, even if you are in (relatively) solid health. Strenuous dancing and running can have disastrous effects on your body if you're not in the proper condition. The last thing you need is to dip a date during the tango and drop her when your shoulder dislocates clean out of the socket. Remember to pack plenty of duct tape before you head out, and reinforce those joints every time you take to the field or floor. You'll thank me later!

ARTS AND CRAFTS
Pottery for Revenants is a nationwide club for those of you with a talent for the arts. Sculpt and throw your very own vases and canopic jars (great for housing leftovers). Just be sure to stay away from the kiln and let a lifer handle the heat.

SPEED DATING
Speed Dating is a fast way to meet the slow moving. Created in 1998 by Rabbi Yaacov Deyo as a means for young marriage-minded Jewish singles to meet, it quickly took off and became the cultural phenomenon it is today. Throwing your own speed dating night is simple and a good way to raise money for your favorite zombie charity. You just need a timer, a bell, and a whole bunch of single undeads.

EVENT(UAL) SUCCESS!
These events and clubs work because they were created with you—a zombie—in mind. No one is going to hold your current life-challenged condition against you. Mentioning your love of preteen runaways and bus-station transients will be met with enthusiastic agreement instead of blowtorches and chain saws. At these affairs, you are free to be you, openly sharing how Polish cleaning ladies make your mouth water and baby's fingers taste good dipped in chocolate, without anyone making a hasty call to the authorities. You'll get a nod of recognition, a wink of understanding, and maybe even make the love connection. Here, you are among friends.

ONLINE MATCHMAKING

The Internet has EVERYTHING, making it statistically probable for you to find a match made in cyberspace heaven. The best part? Connections are lightning fast with no risk of thwacks to the head until meeting face-to-face.

TACKLING THE INTERWEB

If you're of the baby boomer generation you may think you can only meet someone in the traditional manner. Possibly while hunched over a still-struggling victim brought down by a zombie horde, or while clumsily wading through foul, knee-deep water in the sewer system. But fear not! If you can press a button (with a finger, a toe, or whatever digit you have left), you can date online. The technology is intuitive and does more than 80 percent of the work for you.

In this chapter, *Zombie Love* will teach you the do's, don'ts, and it depends of online dating. To get started, you will learn how to test the fetid waters to find out which dating Web site is right for you. Feel free to digitally lurk around other undeads' profiles—you risk zero damage to your already crumbling exterior and can learn a lot about what other people are posting.

BECOMING TECH SAVVY

You'll also learn how to create a dynamic online profile that highlights your virtues. For instance, don't say you're a sprightly, undamaged revenant when in reality you're barely limping by on two desiccated legs. Your date will be nonplussed and will give you negative feedback for the whole cyber world to read. Thumbs down! Instead, you'll discover how to treat this as a positive by saying you're a one-revenant kind of zombie who could never run from commitment.

So come on, don't let the underworld pass you by!

DATING SITES

These are the top Web sites for hooking up and staying in touch. Each one offers something different based on your afterlifestyle. Whatever you're hunting for, there's a site for you!

CATCH.COM

This is the quintessential site that started it all. With hundreds of thousands of users, you can browse both the living and after-living. You may like that it offers a wide variety of individuals to choose from, or you may find it daunting to surf through such a massive dead sea. A handy feature lets you preset parameters, like ethnicity and age at reanimation, when searching for something or someone who will get your heart pumping (if you still had a pulse, anyway).

ZDATE.COM

Started by zombies, for zombies, this site is exclusively for undeads who are serious about getting serious. Zombies on this site are usually goal-oriented with a strong taste for community. So if you're looking for someone to settle down and devour a family with, you'll have way better luck trying what's left of your hand on ZDate than milling around outside some bar.

OKCORPSE.COM

For the young and hip, whose hips still work, this site is geared toward the newly returned who are just sidling up to the all-you-can-eat buffet of the afterlife. Members are looking to go out and grab life, i.e., the living, by the shorthairs and see what happens. So if you just want to get out there and meet new people, find new interests, and taste new body parts, then OkCorpse is your hook-up hot spot.

UNDEAD INTERNET SHORTHAND

2day n01 hs tym 2 typ ot their feelins n plain En. The Internet is full of acronyms, slang, and terms like this that make you want to groan more than normal. They can even make you feel like you don't belong. Nonsense! The Internet is full of zombies looking for acceptance, just like you. If you can face chain saw-wielding breathers every time you go out to eat, you can conquer the Internet. And familiarizing yourself with the terms below will make you a pro in no time. If you come across something online you don't recognize, just Gargle it! You'll be ROTFC (rolling on the floor chomping) in no time.

AnO = Alive 'n' Open: Breathers who like zombies.
BBZ = Big Beautiful Zombie: Ample-bodied revenants.
Beastie = An affectionate term for a best friend who's a zombie.
CwB = Corpses with Benefits. Zombies who only want a hookup.
FM = Fresh Meat: A newly risen zombie or a freshly caught meal.
HAL = Has All Limbs: A reanimate with all limbs still attached.
Humbie = A human who role-plays as a zombie.
IRAL = In Real Afterlife: Offline; in the physical world.
JK = Just Kindled: Recently burned by love or villagers.
KIT = Keep Intact. Usually means they want to stay in touch.
KLR = Karaoke Loving Reanimate. This sings for itself.
LOL = Likes Old Lesions: Okay with advanced decomposition.
MD = Missing Digits. May also mean missing other d-parts.
OMZ = Oh My Zombie!
PSM = Post-Soul Mate. The love of a zombie's afterlife.
Rottie = Hottie zombie. A real looker! Usually with all their limbs.
RR = Recently Reanimated. Meaning within the past year.
TMI = Too Much Immolation: An undead who has been burned by love and/or torches.
WTF = Way Too Fetid: A reanimate who is well past their prime.
Z2Z = Zombie to Zombie: A meeting that takes place offline.
ZF = Zombie Friendly: Usually refers to a place.

MAKE A STELLAR E-IMPRESSION

Facing a blank profile can be daunting. You need to condense all your best attributes down to about two hundred words that will attract cute cannibal corpses and leave them wanting to know more about you. Be honest and avoid embellishing anything too much. Zombies can smell a bloated head a mile away, and unlike a literal bloated head, this is a real turnoff.

YOU

Spotlight your best features, like loyalty, good flesh-finding skills, and a full coating of unrotten skin. Talk yourself up, but exercise a little humility. Or if you're not comfortable tooting your own taps, maybe mention your love of hand-holding—this lets them know you still have hands! Share an amusing anecdote about a recent tandem bike ride through the meat-packing district. They will be able to read between the lines that you've still got arms and legs!

YOUR INTERESTS

Do you enjoy long shambles at dusk along the waterfront, trawling for fresh floaters? Great! Talk about how you would love to have a partner who could help you drag in those water-logged carcasses. List your passions from favorite movies and books to what you think is the choice morsel of a weeping fleshbag. Mention your appreciation for a good sense of humor or how you regularly volunteer down at the soup kitchen by culling the pool of repeat violators of the "No Seconds" rule. There's sure to be another zombie that is on the same putrid plane as you.

PICTURES OF YOU

Pick your most flattering pictures that show off your best side and attributes. Don't post embarrassing ones taken during a night of binge flesheating in the bottom of your crypt, for ghoulish sake! Do show off where you've been and the famous people you've snacked on.

Never put up a pic of you and an ex-breather. And no out-dated pics from when you were freshly reanimated (or worse, still a breather!). You'd just be setting up yourself and that potential something special for a huge disappointment.

WHAT *NOT* TO SAY

Don't get too bogged down in inconsequential details. Leave out the little things, like your love for pigeon meat or distaste for out-of-shape data analysts. A quick overview will suffice for now. Include just enough to allude to great conversations you can have on your first date. That's when you can fill in the gaps of your life story. For example, you may be particularly proud of the time you took out three joggers at once, but think about the impact you'll make when you tell this story face-to-rotting-face. If you write that you find joggers to be a particularly challenging but rewarding meal, your date will be dying all over again to ask you what you mean.

LIGHTS, CAMERA, ACTION!

If you have a little tech know-how and admirable locomotive skills, you may consider creating a video for your dating profile to showcase the breadth of your unlifestyle. Showing that you're undead and proud, your vocal cords still mostly work, and you can confidently wave at the camera without a finger snapping off, proves you've got a limb up on a lot of zombies without you having to say so explicitly. Work it while you've still got it!

However, if graceful movement and discernible speech aren't your strong suits, a video may not be the best route.

VIDEO POINTERS

Shoot in front of a background that will complement your cadaverous, pale visage, like a nice soft blue. Avoid chartreuse and salmon, as they will enhance all those leaky wounds and spreading bruises.

Ambient noise should be avoided, but you can add an underlying tune or theme song to punch up the atmosphere and cover up the incessant cage rattling from your captives. Good picks could be Gounod's "Funeral March of a Marionette" or "Bela Lugosi Is Dead" by the dark wave masters Bauhaus.

Put your camera on a tripod and stand or sit at least three feet away. Too close, and all of your blemishes and missing skin bits will show. What a turnoff! If you have an ax lodged in your gut, shoot from the chest up only…unless you're trying to appeal to something that's into that sort of thing.

TAKE A DEEP, RAGGED BREATH

Be relaxed as an atrophied bag of bones can be. Prepare what you are going to say and do ahead of time, and practice before you start rolling. If your short-term memory isn't up to the job, avoid using clumsy note cards by having a friend hold up cue cards. Once you are filming, remember, you can shoot as many takes as you like and edit together the best material.

HOW WOULD YOU BEST DESCRIBE YOURSELF?

Before you drag and click your personal life into the digital dating pool, be sure you know and accept your reanimated self to the fullest. You're the only one who knows what is festering inside and what deserves to be unleashed to the prospective trundling hordes.

HOLDING UP A MIRROR WITHOUT CRACKING IT

You see yourself as the quintessential country gentleman—thoughtful with a subtle wit and desire for unexpected visitors. But what do others see? Perhaps they see the same, or maybe they see a barn-dwelling loner prone to off-putting non-sequiturs and septic servicemen.

Have you always fancied yourself a Twiggy-thin beauty with a gleaming smile and a lilting laugh? Be careful of this vanity, because others may see a sinewy skeleton with no lips and a frightening, croaking raptor voice.

WHAT DO OTHERS SEE?

As you see, perspective is important. Ask your friends how they see you (if they have eyes) and poll the results for a general overview. Take some time to think about what they say and if they match up with what you consider to be your best traits. Make sure you aren't confusing restraint with laziness or determination for aggression. Then take the quiz on the following page to get a better grasp of your personality as it pertains to dating online. Your results will make you more confident from your first log-in to dead date day.

So go find a pen or pencil, put out a bowl of scabs, and prop up your feet. It's time to learn something new about yourself!

TAKE THE SELF-EVALUATION QUIZ!

Answer *yes*, *no*, or *sometimes* to the following questions.

1. I have a real passion for my afterlife and crawl out of my burrow excited about the day/night ahead.
2. I like getting phone calls.
3. I wish my touch phone didn't require body heat to dial.
4. I like parties.
5. I like to crouch behind the garage at the party-thrower's pad.
6. I find it easy to talk to new people.
7. I find it easier to eat these new people.
8. I treat everyone I encounter with the highest degree of restraint.
9. Then I decide who gets eaten first.
10. Social events energize me.
11. They also make me hungry.
12. I often apply my unnatural reserves of strength to do amazing things, like smashing car windows to get at a lovely collection of day-trippers.
13. I like to be with people.
14. I like people for their brains as well as their bodies.
15. I find puppies, kittens, and infants equally delicious.
16. I enjoy a broad variety of activities that push the limits of my physical and mental capabilities.
17. I feel that I am approachable.
18. I attend to new wounds and infestations immediately.
19. I enjoy helping others.
20. I am hungry.
21. Honesty in a relationship is important to me.
22. It is easy for me to express my real-dead feelings.
23. I control my temper.
24. Unless I'm really hungry.
25. I'm really hungry.

CALCULATING YOUR SCORE

YES = 1 point
NO = 0 points
SOMETIMES = ½ point

0–8 Points

You are a pretty shy zombie. You love to stay home and cuddle with a cutie on a pile of rags and gnaw on some leftover Chinese guy. When you do go out, it's usually to do something low-key, like catch a movie-goer. There's nothing wrong with a solitary afterlifestyle, and you should always be true to yourself, but if you're sick of being solitary alone, then you are the ideal candidate for Internet dating!

9–17 Points

You're about as well-adjusted as a maggot-infested walking cadaver can hope to be. Good for you! You're comfortable in social settings, but you don't have to steal the moonlight. You love a good party, but you don't mind staying in and working on a jigsaw either. Internet dating can certainly work for you, because it will help you shallow down the dating pool and flush out the right creature for you.

18–25 Points

You are about as outgoing as they come! When there's a brain-hungry rampage on an unsuspecting town on misty night, you're one of the leading lurchers. You probably have no problem talking to people, but you might have the tendency to bite their heads off when they try to get a word in edgewise. You may not need Internet dating to meet people, but it might be a good idea to try it so you give others a chance to say something before you cut them off at the knees.

CLUTCH THINGS TO DO *BEFORE* THE DATE

YOU LANDED A DATE! NOW WHAT?

So you met a sexy reanimate at a social shindig—and it knows about your missing ear and unhinged jaw and accepts that questionable repair job on your protruding shoulder. Or you stalked it online and neither party knows what to expect. Either way, who cares?! You're about to embark on your first official romantic encounter.

GET READY

First we'll cover personal grooming, because you have to look sharp to feel confident. You may not have the suaveness of a vampire, but you sure as hell don't want to smell like the rotting ass of a diseased cow. So we've cobbled together a few essential tips that range from filling any non-original holes and cracks to taping up anything that is in jeopardy of falling off. Nothing can spoil a hot date quicker than noxious fluids noisily glopping out onto a theater seat or a loose hand breaking off in someone else's.

GET SET

Next up is etiquette. We'll go over zombified behavior on a first date. What to expect, what to say, and how to act like a perfect gentleman and/or a lady when you're more monster than (wo)man. If you can rise from the dead, so can chivalry!

GO!

Finally, let's plan your perfect first date. It's important to figure out where to go and what to do ahead of time, because a plan will keep the date on course. Think about where to go, what to eat, and appropriate topics of conversation *before* you go out, so you can wow your date with your knowledge on shared interests like brains, brains, brains, and braaaaaaaaaaaaaaaaainnnnsssss instead of worrying over where to go.

PERSONAL GROOMING

We're all in varying degrees of decomposition (even breathers start decaying in their midtwenties). Whether you were reanimated just this morning or have been shambling about the afterlife for decades, nature is taking its course. This doesn't mean you have to accept it.

Hopefully you are one of the lucky ones who was embalmed before the reanimation took hold. With all your natural fluids purged and man-made chemical preservatives in your veins, you've got a fighting chance of looking good for a long while. And if not, well, *Zombie Love* will help you hide your premature decomposition as best as possible.

NO MORE TANGLES?

Hair loss is a drag across both living and undead planes. But it's faster upon reanimation as the follicles shrink and run screaming from your epidermis. Frequent applications of Aqua Net will keep hair in place for the most part, but locking your locks with industrial varnish is a better bet. If you haven't done this already, get on it ASAP, as hair loss will happen at an alarming rate. Choose a timeless style, since you'll be doing this do for a really long time.

When getting ready for a date, spritz a fresh coat of whatever preservative you're using to give your "hair" some added shine. If you've been at it a while with the varnish, you may wish to scrape and chip off your hair to update your look. A fresh do can give you a resurrected sense of confidence! **Caution**: These products are highly flammable. Use discretion.

PLUG IT IN, PLUG IT IN

Another important point to address is the state of your varied orifices. Some, like your mouth, need to remain unsealed and untouched (unless you plan on manually trimming the flesh off the living and breaking it down with an immersion blender). Yes, you will most likely lose the occasional tooth to a shoe kicked in self-defense or an unseen titanium pin holding a joint together. These losses are inevitable and should be expected.

I'm referring to other openings that are more of an "exit" nature than an "entrance." Yes, one or two can serve double duty, but that shall be left to personal preference. Suffice to say that if you weren't born with it (your breather birth, anyway) and you have no plans for using a particular opening, then you need to seal it.

An old-fashioned cork is a quick fix if you're about to leave the hovel, but you should look into something a bit more permanent, such as construction adhesive or latex caulk, for the future. Taking these precautions well in advance will stave off any accidental and embarrassing expulsions, ruining a romantic moment and a fine pair of linen trousers.

YOU DON'T WANT MORE THAN LOVE IN THE AIR

Odors can present their own unique set of problems. Sometimes an air-freshener–lined blazer is enough to do the trick. Who doesn't like that new-car smell? Patchouli can be a nice change, and sandalwood is always pleasant on a summer day. For the autumn and winter months, you can switch between pumpkin spice, evergreen, and cinnamon. Just don't overdo it, or you'll be in danger of drawing too much attention to the fact that you are hiding something.

If you have decomposed to the extent that even janitorial deodorizers are unable to mask your unique scent, then you may have to consider finding yourself a mate with no olfactory organs whatsoever. We all enjoy an adorable button nose or regal Roman profile, but you may have to settle for two gaping holes in a skull if you're overly ripe.

DO YOU HAVE THAT NOT-SO-FRESH FEELING?

There's (almost) nothing that a good rinse and/or flush can't solve. A mixture of warm (never hot!) water, a few tablespoons of Windex, and a splash of white vinegar will take off the majority of those unfortunate oils and leaked emissions. It's not a permanent solution, but it's a great way to prepare for a date.

For added cleanliness, use a good cotton washcloth and an old toothbrush for those hard-to-reach places, but stay away from the steel wool for obvious reasons. You may be tempted to use something a bit stronger. Do not attempt this! You are no longer healing or naturally replacing damaged cells, and harsh solvents can and will permanently ruin what remains of your already frail skin.

FOR REALLY TOUGH GRIME

If your problem is tougher than a rigorous superficial rinsing can handle, you may need to go to the next step. For those of you with only minor deterioration who are still experiencing that unwelcome spoiled feeling, try the formula used by produce sellers to maintain that freshly-harvested look for their fruits and vegetables: a mixture of carnauba, shellac, and beeswax. It seals in all your naturally occurring drippings while keeping out damaging liquids and insects.

Top yourself off with a nice sheen by applying a light coat of spray acrylic polyurethane. It's fairly flexible and transparent and comes in both gloss and matte finishes depending on your personal preference. Just make sure you remove any foreign objects (dust, blood, shrapnel) before applying spray sealant.

IF ALL ELSE FAILS

If you're still experiencing that not-so-fresh feeling, you may still be oozing degenerative juices. As tiny as they are, pores still allow for a certain amount of egress. You can put an end to this once and for all with a Zombie PermaSeal treatment, a complete damming of every opening on your body, other than your mouth and your anus. Even your eyes are propped open and shellacked over, which can leave you with a permanent surprised expression if you're not careful.

Because there are risks with permanent consequences worse than an ill-conceived tramp stamp, you should consider hiring a skilled professional or at least having a friend present to help you avoid the worst pitfalls.

FOUR STEPS TO FEELING FRESH—FOREVER!

For those of you who are going to attempt a PermaSeal yourself, or at least want to know what to expect, here is a step-by-step guide to the process.

1. The first thing you do is prepare the substrate. Remove any loose material and previously applied products such as makeup, tape, Bondo, etc.
2. Fill, patch, and smooth over any remaining cracks, injuries, or orifices using waterproof putty. It will dry hard but still maintain a bit of flexibility for a seminatural look— sort of.
3. Brush on a coat of a waterproof sealer. They only come in white and black, so be careful which one you buy. Once the first layer is dry, apply two more very thin coats, allowing ample drying time in between.
4. Once the final coat is dry to the touch, apply makeup and skin tone paint. This may require an auto-body airbrush, but it's worth the cost for that high-end finish.

A WORD OF CAUTION

Be aware that while you are sealing in all your juices, this does not stop you from decomposing. Now and then, you may want to drill drainage holes in any areas that feel squishy. After you squeeze out the excess, patch the holes with Bondo and reapply the sealant to match the rest of your "flesh."

INOPPORTUNE GASES—YOURS AND THEIRS!

Everybody does it, and there's no real shame in it—just embarrassment. Naturally occurring expulsions/explosions of gas affect all of us on a daily basis. Most try to treat it with some degree of aplomb, but sometimes silent but deadly can be bad, really bad.

THE WHY

As the flesh and interior organs decay (even flesh protected with various varnishes and sealants), they release gases such as hydrogen sulfide, carbon dioxide, and methane—all three of which are extremely odorous. Naturally, they need to go somewhere, and without a proper vent, this can happen in a rather explosive and messy manner.

THE WHEN

It's bad enough when the occasional soft belch or a quiet toot sneaks out on a date, but they are more acceptable than a complete guttural blowout—the consequences of which can be socially and emotionally devastating. Not only will you most likely have destroyed any chance of a future date, you probably ruined your clothes, the table linens, the chair, and the wall behind you. Unfortunately, these explosions often abide by Murphy's Law and erupt as a result of first-date jitters.

THE WHAT TO DO

If you feel that a major eruption is imminent, tactfully excuse yourself and shuffle as quickly as possible to a large shrub for privacy to release your gases, along with whatever else may come out. Unlocked cars are even better, as they muffle the accompanying sounds quite well. If a Dumpster is the only available option, then try to find one that's at least half-full. An empty one will echo embarrassingly and amplify your predicament.

If you are fortunate enough to have a bathroom available, and precious seconds before blowing, then lock the door, run the faucets, and take off your clothes, shoes, and socks (better safe than sorry)! Lay down a bunch of paper toilet seat covers as temporary drop cloths, and create an impromptu levee with layers of TP. Now, you can let 'er rip with confidence!

THE AFTERMATH

Once the expulsions have subsided enough for you to comfortably relax, survey the damage. Be sure to check the walls and ceiling, too. You never know where that stuff is going to land. It is important to clean up after yourself as best as you can. Remember, you're a zombie, not a pig, and your date might have to use the facilities after you.

WHEN YOU WEREN'T THE ONE WHO DEALT IT

If your date is the one who experiences a blowout, try to use some tact. Shield it and its mess as best you can while it cleans up. Any unwanted stares can be stopped by issuing a threatening growl or taking a quick bite out of the nearest offending forearm or ankle.

Be supportive. Your date is far more embarrassed than you, so put on a strong face and help it through the awkwardness—even if most of your energy goes into keeping your own dinner down. Just being there for support and to hold up a tablecloth or a fat guy's torso are all you can do in a situation like that.

If a nasty rupture does occur, chances are the evening's festivities have drawn to a close. Escort your date home and reassure it that while the event was unfortunate, you don't think any less of it—even if you do.

TOP PRODUCTS FOR THE UNDEAD

Lifers have a huge assortment of products they need to keep it all looking good, smelling pretty, and putting it in its place. Reanimates have those needs amplified. Though there's a huge undead market, products targeted to zombies are just starting to trickle into stores. In the meantime, there are some tried-and-true musts for your toolbox.

Here are the things a zombie will always need. Note: The most-beloved product utilized by the undead was and remains duct tape. There is a special section in this book dedicated to it on page 54.

ATTACHMENTS
For making quick fixes on the go, you won't want to get caught without:

- **Krazy Glue.** Great for those little, on-the-go reattachments. Now available in a no-drip tube or pen!
- **Minty Chewing Gum.** A multipurpose product that first freshens your breath and then acts as a small wound plugger-upper.
- **Arrow Fasteners 7/16″ Staples.** The perfect size for those hard-to-grip problem areas.
- **Archie McPhee Bacon Bandages**. Everybody gets boo-boos, and now they can look as yummy as they smell!
- **Keystone Consolidated 14.5 Gauge Bailing Wire.** For those hard-to-contain compound fractures.

COSMETICS
To touch up your look, your smell, or your mangled arm try:

- **Clorox Pine-Sol Disinfectant and Deodorizer.** Funnel into a small atomizer and spritz as needed.
- **Liquitex Acrylic Paint.** A good base cover-up; available in a variety of colors to match any pallor.

- **SC Johnson Wood Paste Wax.** For filling those reoccurring holes, it's small enough to hide in a pocket or open wound!
- **Bonne Bell Lip Smackers Fruit Flavored Lip Balm.** A little trick to help keep those lips looking somewhat human.
- **Baby Wipes.** These are great for cleaning up those emergency spills, splatters, and leaks. They're essential if you're eating ribs and joints.

TOOLS

Here's a short list of very useful instruments that will help you in all shambles of afterlife:

- **Toothpicks.** Because you don't want to get caught with someone's something stuck in your teeth.
- **U-Dig-It Stainless Steel Hand Shovel.** A handy tool for burying any leftovers. Or as the authorities prefer to call them, evidence.
- **Needle-Nose Pliers.** Use to extract small projectiles, like bullets and arrows, or physical snafus, like a dangling tooth and bothersome bone fragments.
- **Nutcracker.** The perfect tool for getting at delicious, hard-to-reach marrow.
- **Pedors Orthopedic Shoes.** You spend a lot of time on your feet/foot, so you should be comfy while stumbling about.

You may find other cannot-unlive-without products that work even better for you. If so, that's great! Please pass the info along if you think it can help others as much as it has helped you. Zombies need to stick together!

THE MIRACLE OF DUCT TAPE

Duct tape deserves a shrine in the zombie hall of fame, and there's a very good reason for that. It's your ultimate, all-around, top-notch fix-it tool. Reliable, portable, and incredibly strong, duct tape now comes in a variety of fashionable colors.

It withstands water, gasoline, and bodily excretions with valor and little limpness. It can be cut to fit just about any orifice or appendage you need to mend and is strong enough to safely secure most dangling extremities, wayward ears, and miscellaneous limbs retrieved from aggressive dogs. And all without the unsightliness of industrial staples or bailing wire. Praise be to duct tape!

MANNERS AND PROPER DATING ETIQUETTE

Manners are just as—if not more—important for the walking dead than for the living. Minor faux pas that could be ignored in life grow exponentially worse in the after. For instance, a tiny shred of scalp stuck between your teeth is *much* grosser than a sliver of spinach. You should always go that extra mile, and an extra trip to the mirror, to make sure you're at your best. You may be dead, but chivalry needn't be!

THE DOS

Cover your mouth. It is imperative you cover your face hole when sneezing or coughing in public. Various bodily fluids are now flowing freely throughout your head and throat, so there's a good chance you're going to blow some serious chunks with each expulsion. Nobody wants to end up with your uvula in their cocktail!

Be complimentary. Zombies need flattery, too, you know. Tell her that her new blouse brings out the lovely green circles around her eyes, or mention that his tie subtly draws attention away from the flies buzzing in and out of his exposed trachea. It may not always be easy to find something to compliment, but as a caring partner you'll always find the good in gangrene. If she lost an arm or a leg to a chain saw, ask her if she's lost weight. If he has a massive shotgun blast to his gut, ask if he's been working out. It's the little things that make the difference.

THE DON'TS

Be agreeable if they don't agree. Though it may have been chivalrous to cover the check or walk a date home in pre-death, doing so now may have its consequences now. Unchecked rage is something all undead have bubbling just below the surface, and anything that can be construed as an insult to one's capabilities threatens to pull off the scab of civility. A gruesome rampage may gush out all over an otherwise pleasant evening if you insist on doing anything your date rejects. Offer politely to pick up the tab, but if your date wants to go dutch, it's best to be agreeable. Otherwise you or your date could easily fall into a gurgling, spewing tirade.

Control Your Urges. If you're on the receiving end of an insistence—for instance your date is the one who is adamant about paying the tab or chasing down dinner—try your best to keep yourself in check. Don't fly into the aforementioned gruesome rampage and tear your date a new one. Politely tell it what you think, and gently let it know that if it does otherwise, you will be uncomfortable. This establishes an honest communication and makes you the better zombie. If you lose your cool, you'll come across as a frothing lunatic who ruined their best outfit.

THE BE-CAREFUL-IF-YOU-DOS
Always move cautiously. Pull out a chair for a female revenant with heed. If you're too hasty, you may accidentally dislodge an already-loose extremity of yours. Too slow, and she may interpret it as advanced decay and assume you're decomposing more quickly than you let on.

Light up at your own risk. Although smoking is generally frowned upon in public, many still enjoy an occasional cigarette or cigar. If you are a fan of the *fumar*, remember that fire is a bane to the undead. Caution cannot be stressed strongly enough. While oozing fluids can keep one fairly well moisturized, a partially mummified undead can flare up like magician's flash paper if hit with a spark.

TABLE MANNERS FOR TABLE-LESS DATES

You will likely experience more than a few dates in less than desirable conditions. Sometimes the linens aren't properly cleaned or the Dumpster was already picked over by raccoons. You may find that your once-favorite place for dinner has segregated seating that you find insulting.

AFTERLIFE'S A PICNIC

If you end up in a neighborhood outside of your comfort zone, why not make an adventure out of it by turning the date into a picnic? It may sound a little crazy, but a great way to show your "creative" side is by taking down some nuns and using their habits as a picnic blanket.

Make the makeshift picnic fun! Drudge up a discarded box, throw a little twine through the top, and you've got the basket. Half-empty bottles of flat soda or hubcaps filled with tepid rain water, and voilá, you have a delectable dinner beverage. Then scavenge the alleys behind restaurants, bars, and pet stores, and you'll find any number of leftovers and expired stock to add to your box of goodies.

GRABBING A QUICK BITE

Not every date should be a hunt for delicious living flesh. Sure, it's a great activity you both enjoy, but sometimes it's nice to be able to sit down and talk (or gurgle, as the case may be)—especially in the beginning when you're getting to know each other. Retirement villages are excellent places to grab a quick bite. The inhabitants are slower moving than you, and a lot of the time they won't even be able to see you coming!

GOOD DATE SPOTS

While on your way to your romantic dinner, you may find yourselves in the unenviable position of being hounded by a mob of angry fleshbags intent on your destruction. While this will make for a great story if you survive, right now you need to focus on getting away from the intolerant rubes. Get to side streets and wooded areas as quickly as possible, since large mobs have a difficult time navigating them. And by no means stop for dinner! Get out of their sights and find a place to hide until they pass, *then* grab one of the slow walkers as a victory snack.

NO-TABLE MANNERS

Many after-death dinner dates are not sit-down affairs. Since you'll often be sans table, it's important you try to find a safe, comfortable spot while still employing the imperative rules of etiquette.

You won't have a napkin, so use some leaves or your meal's shirt. Unless you maintained preparedness lessons from your scout days, you'll probably be utensil-less. The polite thing to do is fashion some quick stakes out of sticks or bicycle spokes. You still need to stand if your date needs to excuse itself from the feeding area, but on the plus side, you won't have to deal with the embarrassment of mixing up the salad and dinner fork!

FOR A HAPPY ENDING . . .

Always let your date have the last piece. This may be difficult because of the intense power of your hunger for tasty, tender tendons, but for the love of all things unholy, keep it at bay! If you bare your teeth and gnash your jaws at your date, chances are you won't be asked out again, and you may even find yourself locked in a choke hold. However, if you keep your appetite in check, then your date will admire your willpower, and you could find yourself locked in a different sort of hold for dessert.

EAT THIS, NOT THAT

A great way to impress your companion while out to dinner is by knowing which wine or spirit best complements a cut of meat. Oozing fluids, stomach acids, and puddled rainwater are usually acceptable beverages, but if you pair with panache and class, you'll stand out above their previous zombie dates. Here's an aid to help you bone up before you go out.

The chuck cut (shoulders, upper chest) is a delectably lean piece of meat. While it doesn't have the well-marbled flavoring of a sirloin, it still has its charms. It can be a bit stringy if ripped from a slender victim (a runner or wiry Floridian), but if paired with a lukewarm Mr. Pibb or aged spleen-squeezings it makes a hearty and memorable meal.

The flank cuts (outer shoulders, upper and inner thighs) provide a denser, heavier meal that may not appeal to everyone's palette. Lightly marbled, it takes less of its flavor from surrounding fat, and thus its unique charm comes from its inherent "gaminess." It is best ingested in smaller, fist-sized pieces and is complemented nicely by leaking engine coolant or the tepid, mosquito-laden water resting in the bottom of an old tire.

The sirloin and short plate (sides, abdomen) are well-marbled cuts from little-used muscle groups and are thus the most tender and easy to dislodge. They lack any strong taste or distinct flavor but carry their natural juices well and are perfect for even the most sensitive palate. These cuts go particularly well with a fine single-malt scotch, port, or rancid bile.

The groin is a cut of meat that, along with the sweetbreads, is an acquired taste for many. It varies from gender to gender and meal to meal and thus is quite unpredictable. A rich Bordeaux makes a good pairing, as it can compensate for a less palatable

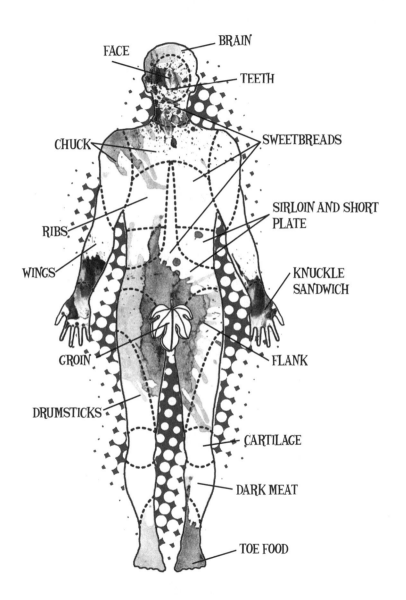

meat. Also, use discretion—diving into the groin on a first date may send the wrong message.

Sweetbreads refers to several distinct body parts: The throat and gullet sweetbreads and the heart and pancreas sweetbreads. Considered a delicacy, they are called sweetbreads since that sounds a little tastier than calling them guts, offal, or crap factory. A decanter of windshield cleaner or a saucer of spinal fluid both make a fine partnering.

Anything above the neck is questionable unless you're referring specifically to the eyes (delicious jelly candies) or better yet, the braaaaiiinnnns. The face, hair, lips, and ears are fine for a snack, but they are not enough for a proper meal. Either brittle or full of cartilage, these pieces can be difficult to chew, especially if you've lost your jaw or most of your teeth. Strong drink goes best with this food group. Isopropyl alcohol, paint thinner, or anything with uric acid is recommended.

The brain is without a doubt the most delicious and prized piece of meat you can harvest for a meal. Once you manage to break through its protective case (be careful not to damage the lobes, as they're quite delicate), carefully scoop out this treasure onto a cracked Spode serving platter. Really, nothing screams classy better than this! The brain (especially the cerebellum and the hard-to-reach temporal lobe) is best served when warm and wet, complemented with a delicate pinot noir or flat ginger ale to bring out the natural flavors.

PLANNING THE PERFECT FIRST DATE

Are you looking for a simple, quiet get-together where the two of you can learn about each other? A local coffee shop with the delicious-looking baristas is nice, as is a good old stalk in the park. With so many options at your bony fingertips, the perfect date spot just depends on your taste.

SOMETHING SIMPLE

If you're still in the early phases of your relationship, it's good to keep things simple and modest. Small dinners in quiet restaurants, a picnic in a secluded area of the park, or a romantic stroll behind the scrap metal yard by the docks all offer appropriately intimate surroundings for your tête-à-tête.

You may also wish to consider a quiet shamble through a moonlit cemetery or a pre-dawn exhumation. Both offer some alone time accompanied by Mother Nature's beauty. Just be sure to finish up your activities before those early-morning runners interrupt you. Unless, of course, those are your intentions. Yum!

SOMETHING MEMORABLE

If you want to make a lasting impression on your first date, you may want to skip cozy for something like a concert or a trip to the local flea market. Spending your time with others is a great way to see how your date interacts with the living and shows them that you can exhibit a tasteful level of restraint in public. Few things are more embarrassing than having your partner lurching at some breathers, spraying them with toxic saliva, thus getting you both kicked out of a Slayer concert. But on the other hand, you don't want something who doesn't pounce on a good opportunity, like some doughy groupies who didn't make it backstage after the concert.

HAPPENINGS AND HOT SPOTS

Here is a list of can't-miss places to go and spot-on things to do. These are great for every stage of relationship and decomposition.

- **The Zoo.** Packed with exotic snacks! But watch out for the primates—for some reason they really freak out around the undead.
- **County Fair.** Great rides and fun food.
- **The Museum.** Educational—just don't end up as one of the exhibits.
- **Habitat for Humanity Build.** Charitable people tend to have a sweet taste, and their meat is very giving.
- **A Concert.** Perfect for blending in with the crowd, especially if you're attending a GWAR show or seeing a Misfits cover band. Pass on the Josh Groban concert for now.
- **Amusement Parks.** Most enjoyable during Halloween events throughout the fall, you will probably fit right in with costume-clad employees. Make sure any rides you go on have ample safety restraints, and you keep your limbs inside the cars at all times!
- **Zombie Walks.** You'll be a shoo-in for "Best Costume."
- **Garage Sales.** Good for sizing up your neighbors and finding a new-to-you dining table!
- **Fireworks Displays.** Romantic from afar—deadly up close!
- **Game Night.** Playing a few rounds of manhunt is an excellent way to show off your stalking skills, but avoid Twister so no one loses a loose leg to an elusive red dot.
- **Food Pantry.** Thinning out the numbers of visitors will ensure that the ones who make it inside are well fed, and your date will surely admire your charitable nature.

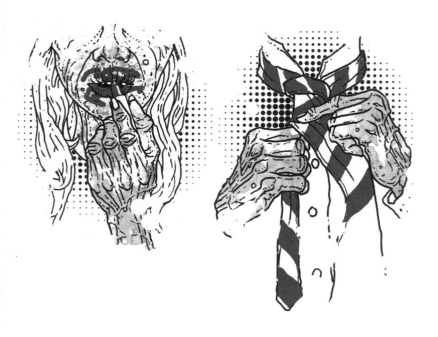

WHAT TO WEAR

Plan your attire according to the date. Go too casual, and your date may feel that you don't care enough to look your very best. Too formal and you risk the possibility your date will think you're a stuffed shirt or that you had to stuff your shirt to hide some gangrenous holes.

DON'T OVER THINK IT

Use common sense and let the venue dictate your attire. If you're meeting up for a simple coffee and a light bite, then casual but neat is the rule. Quickly spot-treat those foul stains that speckle the front of your khakis and be sure to pick off any stray hairs and bits of throat left over from breakfast.

A lunch meet-up allows for more leeway, as that meal presents a variety of possibilities. If you are (or were) a man, you can sport the informal look of a tucked polo shirt and Dockers for that quick nosh in the alley behind your favorite deli. If you're planning on dining al fresco in back of that all-the-rage French bistro, then a sport coat is a must. A tie is not required, but a structured informality is de rigueur. Or rigor mortis, depending on your state of decay.

For the ladies, a skirt is always nice, no matter how informal the event. A blood-free blouse or light sweater and matching shoes are sure to impress your date. But check your hose—you may have destroyed them while running down a nurse on her shift break.

DRESS TO IMPRESS—OR AT LEAST NOT DISGUST

As one of the undead, you probably do not have the greatest wardrobe. While your date may be able to sympathize with you, you still need to try your best. You certainly don't want to see your date in the same torn, bloodied, and tissue-covered clothes time and again, and most likely it doesn't want to see you in the same soiled outfit every date either. Build yourself a flexible array of attire, and you'll always have something that fits the mood on any occasion.

Shoes are a very important element to any good wardrobe. A few pairs of loafers and oxfords for men or a selection of comfortable flats and low heels for women is a great start. Try to stay with material that cleans easily. Leather is always great, and it also makes an acceptable snack if you get locked in a cellar for an indeterminate amount of time.

WHERE TO SHOP

Resale and consignment shops work really well for finding quality garments that don't break the bank. The Salvation Army and Goodwill are excellent resources not only for your day-to-day wear, but they are also perfect places to look for jewelry, belts, and other accessories. It's easier to accept the loss of $5 purse than a twice-used $125 Fossil bag ruined by leftover innards salad.

MOST IMPORTANTLY

The key to the right outfit is that it makes you both comfortable and confident. Fussing with a waistband that's digging into your open sores all night is a drag for you, and your date is sure to notice. Assume that it is planning on looking its best for you, so you should be just as considerate.

THE ALTERNATIVE

If you are pretty far down the musty trail of decay, you may just want to embrace that you've been around the chopping block a few times. Wear your favorite tattered rags that stink of rancid meat, leave the ocular bits on your one remaining boot, and never mind your shredded underwear. If you think your date can handle it, try reveling in your stank and gore—you may just bring out its predator instincts and find yourself having a wild night!

BEATING BACK AN ANGRY HORDE OF NERVES (AND POSSIBLY VILLAGERS)

First-, second-, and even third-date jitters affect almost everyone. Sure, you've agreed to the date, but what now? How do you deal with the butterflies (or in your case, just flies) in your stomach? No matter what you do or who you end up eating, don't let your deteriorating nerves get the best of you.

Remember that it is OK to be a little anxious. It shows that you care, and that's a good thing. Plus, your date is likely to be just as nervous and apprehensive as you, so there's no reason to drive yourself into an unwarranted panic.

While you have lost some of the qualities that made you human—like empathy, pity, and the ability to make a decent cup of coffee—it's important to hang on to whatever you can. That said, you may find a certain amount of nervousness before a date exhilarating. The main thing is that you don't let it get the best of you. You do not want to be sitting across from your date with a sweat-coated skull and trembling hands, sputtering incoherent nonsense. Leave that to your next meal!

HOW TO TAKE THE EDGE OFF

If your respiratory system is still capable of pumping air, try this simple but effective breathing exercise: Inhale deeply through your nose (if intact), and slowly exhale through your mouth (or what passes for one). Even though you no longer need to breathe, this familiar motion, done with intention, will focus your rampaging thoughts on something other than the mental image of a stray dog crashing your date, chomping down on a dangling bit of your innards, and running off down the road with one end of your intestines in his mouth. The odds of that happening are extremely statistically insignificant! So take a half-dozen deep breaths, and you should start feeling a bit more relaxed. Stop if you begin to feel dizzy or cough up a piece of lung or a loose tooth.

WORST CASE SCENARIO

But what do you do if a dog *does* come along and mistakes you for a giant Milk Bone? Or what if a horde of angry villagers chooses the night of your first date to seek vengeance on the undead for making gazpacho out of their brains and heirloom tomatoes one too many times? These ugly possibilities will always a source of anxiety for revenants, but they can be particularly panic-inducing when you're already nervous about creating the perfect evening for you and your paramorgue.

The best way to feel at peace with these possibilities is to be prepared. Make sure any loose bits are tightly secured inside your body cavity using duct tape. Carry a few easily concealed weapons, such as a can of Mace or rusty barbed wire to wrap around your knuckles. And always remember that you're the one with the toxic gaping maw, so they are more afraid of you than you are of them.

DON'T DRIVE DRUNK DOWN THE EASY ROAD

Some folks try to reduce tension with a muscle relaxer or even a couple shots of isopropyl rubbing alcohol to take off the edge and reduce their anxiety. This is not recommended. It will affect your already-reduced faculties. You could turn into a slobbering, uncoordinated hot mess—more so—and end up ruining any future you may have had with your date by presenting an unattractive side of yourself—less so. To put it bluntly, you're a rotting corpse, so don't do anything that may hurt your chances even further.

DON'T LEAVE THE DEN WITHOUT IT!

There are a few things and parts you absolutely need to make sure you have before you head out for your big date. Here are a few must-haves to ensure that your date is a tragedy to remember:

Reservations. Few things make a date go awry faster than getting to the restaurant only to discover they're booked, or "booked" as the case may be for zombies.

Cash. It's always good to carry some moola and some plastic, so you can pick up a bouquet of rose stems or bribe some rowdy street thugs into giving back your arm if their numbers prevent you from delivering some heated zombie justice unto their punk asses.

Cinnamon gum or breath mints. The last thing you want your date to notice is your last meal. Nothing covers the smell better than Big Dead.

Fresh underwear. Because your mother told you to never leave the house wearing dirty underwear, and that advice has never been more relevant than it is now.

Floss. For those quick dental touch-ups, because nothing is more off-putting than a missed bit of intestine or stray scrap of clothing.

Duct tape. For securing those loose bits, this truly is the undeads' best friend.

Deodorant and toothbrush. In case you don't make it home tonight, tiger!

Skin and Limbs. He doesn't need to see you without your face on yet, and she will want to know you're endowed—if only prosthetically.

THE ART OF DATING

IS THERE AN "ART" TO DATING?

Art is typically defined as the expression or application of human creative skill and imagination to any given medium. Now, putting aside the somewhat bigoted use of the word "human," can we apply the word "art" to the various machinations employed when dating? I believe we can. If you're one of the dating-undead, you'll quickly discover it takes both skill and imagination to pull off a successful night out. *Zombie Love* can help you hone your talents and become a master of the form.

BE CREATIVE AND FLEXIBLE

Even the best laid plans of mice and zombies oft go awry. Though planning your date is a prerequisite, it takes some charm and finesse to make a date a good one when it is derailed by circumstance or yokels out of your control.

For the undead it is crucial to have grace under fire—but hopefully not literally. Say you arrive at a restaurant only to discover your reservations have been cancelled since a revenant just ate the chef's grandmother. It will require some quick, creative thinking on your part to come up with a new plan. You will also need a degree of flexibility (not so easy for the rigor-mortis-afflicted) to escape through the service entrance while being pursued by an angry man with knife skills.

Sometimes things start off smoothly but then go wrong over dinner. What if your date loses an appendage under the table in a poorly played game of footsie, or you gamble with a fart and lose? There's real value in the ability to take an embarrassing situation and paint it in a positive light.

PERFECTING THE ART

As with all art, your skills will improve over time and with practice. The more dates you go on, the more comfortable you will become. And with *Zombie Love* to help train you, you will be a true renaissance zombie in no time!

THE DREAM FIRST DATE

You've got your best activity-appropriate outfit on. You've shel-lacked, puttied, glued, taped, painted, and perfumed your various parts and holes. You've devised a lively, no-pressure date (with plenty of exit strategies). You've done your pre-date due diligence, but even with all this prep work, things can go off track. Though you can't control all circumstances, there are some general do's and don'ts that will help things run as smoothly as fate will allow.

THE DO'S

Be on time. It is *critical* to be punctual on a first date. It shows that, even as a maggot-filled corpse, you are excited for the meet-up and pretty dang courteous. If you're late, your date will start the evening annoyed, not to mention you left them alone, exposed to zombie-hating breathers.

Be cool, be yourself. It's important to act relaxed and like yourself—no matter how nervous you may be. You want it to get to know the real you, so be honest. This will save you from a lot of backpeddling over trapdoors later.

Be polite—to everyone. We already covered the chivalry thing, but remember to also be well-mannered to anyone you encounter. If you are rude to the waitress, greedily devour a movie-ticket taker without offering to share, or are dismissive to a barista, how does that make you look? Like a monster—and you certainly don't need to go inviting that comparison.

Turn off your phone! When that telltale jingle rings in your pocket, it screams to your date that it is not your priority. So instead of turning off your honey by having your Michael Jackson "Thriller" ringtone interrupt its story, turn off your phone!

THE DON'TS

Don't be a pig. As one of the walking dead, your hunger is an insatiable, ravenous force that consumes you with the same urgency with which you consume your prey. It is your challenge to remain reasonably in control. Don't let dinner turn into a snarling, gnashing affair where you fight over the temporal lobe. Take it easy, and give your date first dibs. Your restraint will be rewarded in the end with a high opinion. A good trick: Eat before you go!

Don't assume you have the same sense of humor. What's funny to one may not be a knee-slapper to another. It's best to hold off on the off-color jokes until you know your zombie love's sensibilities a little bit better. If you are burning to tell a joke to lighten the mood, then err on the side of propriety. Avoid potentially repelling jokes like, "Why did the zombie cross the road? To eat the stroller full of fresh, delicious babies on the other side," and stick with the universal, "Do zombies eat popcorn with their fingers? No, they eat their fingers separately."

Don't ooze desperation. Try not to come across as pathetically lonely. It is a major red flag. Never say you really want to get married ASAP or that you really want children before you get much moldier. This will frighten off your date quicker than a well-armed militia. Save that talk until after you know you can stand each other for more than one night!

Don't mention your health issues. Your date doesn't yet need to know that your genitalia are missing or that your bowels are being kept in place with sawdust and wax. These issues may be weighing heavily on you (or not, as the case may be), but your date doesn't need to that because . . .

Don't sleep together on the first date! No matter how well it goes, sex on the first date is rushing something that you should have the chance to salivate over for a bit.

WHAT TO SAY AND WHAT NEVER TO SAY

There are few things more painful on a first date than that awkward silence that sets in like tuberculosis when you're both at a loss for words. You know how it goes—the harder you try, the more difficult it becomes, even when both your mouths are fully functioning.

The breaks between sentences grow longer as the conversation deteriorates quicker than your flesh on a Dallas sidewalk in July. Awkward, toothy grins and eyes nervously darting about replace relaxed smiles and romantic glances. Eventually you find yourself frantically looking around the room for something of interest to buoy the dying conversation, and before you know it, you're covered in flop sweat and making inane comments about the light fixtures or asking your date how they get those really tough lower GI stains out of their clothes.

AVOIDING DEADLY SILENCES

Planning a few can't-miss topics ahead of time is a surefire way to make sure the night keeps a lively tempo. Before your date, spend a few minutes reading the paper or surfing the Web to see what's going on in the current worlds of art, music, and entertainment.

This will help you open up a chat about the latest movies: What did they see, and why did they like it? Was there enough gnashing and chewing to fit their taste, or was there really nothing in it for them to sink their teeth into?

Perhaps there is a new exhibit at the museum or a rock show at the nightclub. Has it heard of the artist? Does it want to go check out the show and then ambush the artist after-hours if the performance lacks sustenance? This is also is an easy way to ask for another date!

KNOW BEFORE YOU GO

Think about what you would like to share about yourself. Start easy—music, movies, books—before you go for the jugular—religion, politics, human veal. Try to keep these topics as open-ended as possible. Avoid yes-or-no answers; otherwise you run the risk of turning the conversation into an interview. Delve a little deeper for the why or why not.

Try to bring the conversation back around to your date to show that you're interested. Perhaps you'll discover that you share the same embalmer or that your mothers went to the same grade school—you never know!

AVOIDANCE IS OK

Unless you know you agree with (or can at least tolerate) your date's opinions, you should avoid discussing politics or religion on a first date. Nothing can turn a pleasant conversation into a snarling debate quicker than two people disagreeing on those very sensitive topics!

You may also wish to avoid the delicate topic of life-on-death dating. Faux pas! Ultimately you will want to know their opinions on these issues, but there's no reason to spoil an otherwise unlively connection with irrelevant rhetoric.

GO WITH IT

In reality, you are still discovering who or what the other person-like thing is. You're not comfortable enough to just sit in silence and enjoy each other's consumption; it will take time before you reach this point. But as long as the date is moldering in a positive fashion, you can relax and just go with the blood flow.

WHAT TO DO IF THINGS GO OFF THE RAILS

Sometimes even the best dates can unexpectedly misfire and go astray, injuring innocent bystanders. Wounds ooze, exes show up unexpectedly, ambushes happen. If something bad does go down, don't panic. Just follow these guidelines.

SURVEY THE DAMAGE
There are varying degrees of "off the rails," and you need to know where and why the derailment happened in order to get the date back on track as quickly and smoothly as possible.

First, stay calm and evaluate the situation. Is anybody crying? How about screaming? Is your date silently seething with resentment or simply at a loss for words? Are there body parts anywhere? Are there body parts everywhere? Whose are they? Once you figure out the problem, you can start to fix it. Or cut your losses and run.

DAMAGE CONTROL
If you made a conversational misstep, like a glib pro-afterlife statement to a battle-ready pro-lifer, switch topics pronto. Mention how much you enjoyed the appetizers, or compliment it on its thick skull. Don't go overboard; just use enough to pull the corpse out of the funeral pyre.

Some blunders are harder to recover from. Say for instance you mistake a waiter with a blowtorch coming to fire your crème brâin for a rampaging, zombie-hating, son-of-a-bitch breather. Instincts kick in and as you rip him a whole host of new ones, you accidentally splatter some bile on your date's new dress. Not good. For a faux pas this size, all you can do is apologize. An honest and sincere "I'm sorry" can go a long way, and you just need it to take you far enough for your date to calm down and see you meant well.

KNOW WHEN NOT TO RESUSCITATE

There are times when the evening is too far gone to resurrect. Somehow over the course of a few short hours your date has deteriorated from a pleasant night out into a frothing mess from which you are desperately trying to escape.

It might be hard to tell when it started to skid off the runway into the ditch or pinpoint when exactly it burst into flames. An unexpected silence or awkward stare may be the only indication that something you said or did set it all off. Or maybe you don't need the black box to know the whole thing combusted when you went to romantically stroke her hair and broke off a carefully sculpted layer and the only ear she had left.

No matter what you or your date did, you can always tell the night is over by identifying three simple signs:

1. Eye contact is more awkward than the time you accidentally mouth-kissed your aunt when you were going for cheek.
2. If given the option, you'd rather be scrubbing mystery stains off the wall of a bus station bathroom than order dessert.
3. The place is on fire, there's blood everywhere, a terrified fat woman is crying in the corner, and you're not even enjoying it.

CALL IT QUITS

If a date has ground to a screeching halt, it may be tempting to stick it out for politeness's sake. But if someone has been offended, a cold, uncomfortable silence can quickly lead to a lunge across the table, spilled viscera, and a ruined suit. In the world of undead dating, your best bet is to take a deep breath and admit that things aren't working out. Odds are it is thinking the same thing. Just lead with a compliment, don't place blame, and—to be on the safe side—run like hell.

TO KISS OR NOT TO KISS?

If your cold palms are sweating and you find yourself falling deeper into their ocular cavities, you may have found a meaningful connection. If you're this lucky, a kiss is definitely in order. However, you need to ascertain a few things before going in for that very first lip-lock.

WHOSE LIPS ARE THOSE, ANYWAY?

Does your partner even *have* lips? If so, are they well-secured to its face or dangling dangerously by a few remaining strands of decayed tissue? If they don't look like they can withstand any more action than they've already seen, err on the side of caution. Go for a solid hug, a lingering kiss on their cheek—or whatever remaining facial tissue you can find—and hope your date takes the lead from there.

TREAD LIGHTLY

If you've determined that your date's lips are sensuously ready, go ahead and make your move. You don't want to come away with more in your mouth than you went in with, so take it easy at first. A light peck, no tongue (out of propriety and not knowing the constancy of that attachment), with only a little movement to test for tensile fortitude.

It may seem like thinking about all this stuff puts you in danger of sapping some romance out of the moment, but there are few worse ways to end a great night than with your date's lips hanging off yours like so much rotten sashimi.

WHAT IF IT DOESN'T HAVE ANY LIPS?

If its features have decomposed to the extent that you're moving in on something that resembles a sexy mako shark, don't fret. There's nothing that says you can't run your mouth muscle over a row of exposed teeth. Of course it won't feel that tender, but this new sensation will make it all the more memorable.

GOING STEADY

You and your partner have been together now for a while and things are purring along nicely. When you're together the sun feels warmer, the birds sing more sweetly, and the blood flows more freely. You've found love, and nothing can stand in your way. The only thing that can ruin it for you now is you.

THAT FLUTTERY FEELING IN YOUR GUTS

You've found that perfect guy/gal/ghoul, and you are crazy about each other. All you want to do is be with them. It's understandable that you're feeling this way, but don't let love veil your eyes from seeing potential pitfalls. Have you heard the old adage "familiarity breeds contempt"? What about "absence makes the heart grow fonder"? How does "nothing festers in the shade" strike you?

The point is that through constant exposure to someone or something, the awe, infatuation, and mystery lessens. It's just how it is. Right now there's an excitement; you get moths in your gut when the two of you are on the prowl searching for that lone paperboy or power walker. The last thing you want is for those pre-dawn feastings to become just another meal before you have the chance to grow deeper feelings of trust and commitment.

SLOW AND STEADY

What you need to do at this point is make sure you're taking it slow enough. That's not to say you should break dates and become standoffish and emotionally distant. You should still offer it firsties on any fresh kills or newfound brainpan. You still need to be you—thoughtful, courteous, and attentive. You just need to try to hit that meaty spot where you see each other enough for the relationship to grow but not so often that it becomes boring and routine. You've got a whole afterlifetime for that!

Instead of seeing that special thing every other day, try twice a week for the first couple of months. It will help make the time you do spend together even more special. Instead of a whole weekend of routine activities interspersed with random feedings, how about planning one long day overflowing with adventure, capped off by a innovative dinner in Chinatown?

BUILDING MOMENTUM

By seeing each other less in the beginning, you will appreciate each other all the more. But if you spend too much time together too soon, the flame dies before it has the chance to burst into a lasting fire. Instead of feeling giddy anticipation to see them, you feel a burden snowballing like too much indigestible hair.

But if you start by seeing each other only when you have a fun activity or special event planned and then let your lives naturally feed into each other, you've got the foundation of a solid relationship. Soon you'll go from a weeknight dinner date and a weekend tryst to finding you've got a happy hour you want her to crash with you on Tuesday, a ballroom dancing class you both like stalking on Thursday, then Friday tops off the week with the classic date night. Though the moths in your large intestine are no longer fluttering, they've been replaced by a seeping sensation of contentment that fills in all your cracks and crevices.

TO BRING A BOUQUET OR SOMETHING SQUIRMING?

You like it, it likes you. You're becoming more relaxed with each other all the time. The relationship has grown from midnight attacks on lone city workers or inebriated longshoremen to something much more substantial. Now you're dying to get your sweetie something that shows it how you feel, but what should that thing be?

SAY THE RIGHT THING . . .

The best way to test the waters for something deeper lurking under the clotted surface is by giving a small token of your affection. You want to show your dear that it means something to you, but you're afraid to send the wrong message. You don't want to scare it off with a gift that says you're getting too serious too early, but you also don't want to give it something that says, "This rancid squirrel I found under a Dumpster made me think of you." Unless of course you met while indulging your guilty pleasure of rancid squirrel under a Dumpster.

. . . WITH THE RIGHT GIFT

Start small. Inexpensive but thoughtful presents can go a long way for opening the door to the squalid chunk of muscle in their chest. Instead of splurging on a $200 bouquet of roses, opt for the meaningful single red rose still grasped in its former owner's stiffened hand.

Perhaps during your last date he dribbled a big splotch of gravy on his favorite tie. Surprise him with a new one you stitched yourself using clothing you ripped off a terrified tailor in the garment district. If it once told you in passing that its guilty pleasure was watching reality TV, imagine how impressed it would be at your thoughtfulness if you were to bring it Jon Gosselin's head in a duffel bag or, even better, one of the Kardashians'?

THE NEXT LEVEL

Once you've broken the gift-giving ice you can move up to the pricier items, if you're still so inclined. Bracelets, necklaces, and watches are among the nicest jewelry items to gift, but avoid rings so you don't jump the shotgun and send any signals that could be misinterpreted.

Both reanimated women and men appreciate a high-end accessory. For her, a nice leather purse or tote you crafted from an ample-bodied Italian is thoughtful and practical. For him, consider a new stingray-skin wallet or belt made from the finest Parisian intestine. With those classy items, he'll have all the confidence he had before that fox ran off with his fibula. And if you're ever at a loss for what to give, you can never go wrong with brains!

YOU'RE IN!

No matter what you decide to go with, if it's met with a delighted gasp and a twinkle under the milky film of your special some-thing's eyes, then you're golden! You've given it a symbol of your feelings, and it has happily accepted it. You may even get a reciprocal gift. But if you don't get one, don't let it rustle your rags. Feelings are not always expressed the same way—and maybe its style is to send sweetly sour text messages or make sure you get first crack at dozing bums. Don't worry; if it's into you, too, you'll know!

TOP 10 DATE MOVIES

Treat your sweetie to a night in with these fun flicks. You will be sure to get some chuckles and some tears as you make your way through these undead classics.

1. *The Return of the Living Dead* (1985)
   A perfect rom-com for that couple just learning about each other's tastes.

2. *Dawn of the Dead* (1978)
   Materialistic shoppers are shown the error of their fleshsack ways in this hilarious action-adventure!

3. *Old Yeller* (1957)
   A tearjerker that captures the sorrow of having to put down a member of a family who has contracted a rare affliction.

4. *Shaun of the Dead* (2004)
   A well-written small-town drama about a tight-knit but vicious circle of friends. Not recommended for those with a weak stomach.

5. *Sex and the City* (2008)
   An exhilarating and reaffirming film that follows the loves and adventures of four fully-functioning, slightly-deteriorated reanimated corpses as they creep and totter around Manhattan in search of fresh meat.

6. *Fido* (2006)
   Light but tender fare about the bond between a zombie and his boy.

7. *Titanic* (1997)
   For the seafood lovers out there, Leo and Kate are a tasty pair of dreamboats!

8. *White Zombie* (1932)
   A historical documentary featuring the sexy Bela Lugosi and Madge Bellamy.

9. *The Naked Prey* (1966)
   A nude, unarmed human is released in the wild and hunted. What else need be said?

10. *Night of the Living Dead* (1968)
    A lush period piece about the familial discourse between a playful brother (Johnnie) and his arrogant and status-driven sister (Barbra).

WHAT FEM-ZOMBIES WANT AND WHAT THEY NEED

Since the dawn of civilization, women have been an enigma to men. Somewhere, painted on the walls of the Lascaux caves, there's an image of a Paleolithic man scratching his head out of frustration, not sure what he did wrong.

While there are no definitive answers to all of man's questions regarding the needs and wants of the fairer sex, there are a few basic rules that need to be followed if you want to make your afterlife a whole lot easier.

IT/SHE WANTS IT

It wants compliments—it is more ravenous for them than it is for a basement full of World of Warcraft nerds. So serve 'em up! Even if you're one of those beings who feels awkward dripping some honey, do it anyway! Comment on its beauty and sex appeal—even though it recently lost its arm to a freight elevator door. Hotter yet is that makeshift limb it fashioned out of PVC, pleather, and driftwood, that clever girl-like zombie! Say only things you mean, and say them more often than after screwups and anniversaries.

IT/SHE CAN'T UNLIVE WITHOUT IT

Making it feel secure is a must. It wants to know that you're not going to leave it for that hot little recently reanimated number that just moved into the sewer drain down the street. Hold hands, cuddle, and spoon—you'll soon learn that actions that may seem like they're just for her/it at first are fun for both of you.

Ultimately, it needs someone to be there for it, to support it emotionally, physically, and spiritually. It needs you to rub its tired feet at the end of a long day, stroke its nettled hair, and patch that recent hatchet wound that's infuriatingly out of its reach.

WHAT MEN-ZOMBIES WANT AND WHAT THEY NEED

Men-zombies aren't nearly as complex or introspective as the AfterLifetime Channel would lead one to believe. The needs of most zombie dudes are generally pretty basic: food, sleep, sex, and shelter in a vacant warehouse. Their emotional needs are few, and usually they are satisfied if you let them do their own thing instead of having things done for them.

IT/HE WANTS IT

It wants to feel like it's in charge. Even if you're the one with two functioning legs, it'll insist on trying to take down the young lady training for a 5K. Let it try, and don't make a big hoopla out of making it feel better if it fails. It happens to all undead at some point, and it's better to blow past it than harp on it.

It wants some variety. One week it may be interested only in spicy Latinas, and the next it's chasing Asian girls at the mall. Tastes change, so let it have its fun. As long as the two of you still enjoy your traditional twice-weekly meal of Swedes, you have nothing to worry about.

IT/HE CAN'T UNLIVE WITHOUT IT

It needs to be in the company of other bros every once in a while. It may be difficult to understand why sometimes it would prefer to hole up in some dank sewer playing spades with its buddies than snuggle with you on the couch and watch the new episode of *Zombie Shore*, but by giving it a little freedom you will ensure it's happy at home.

When it is home, it wants a place to call its own. Whether it chooses an overstuffed corpse in front of the TV or a man-zombie-cave excavated beneath the garage, it needs its space. The hidey-hole doesn't have to be much, just big enough where it can comfortably retire and be alone with its thoughts—or lack thereof.

INTIMACY

S-E-X. Not quite a four-letter word, but in today's society it's certainly treated like one. As an undead, you may have the same amount of questions you had during your budding pubescence as a lifer, but now they are about bubbling putrescence. It was embarrassing enough to fumble around, figuring out how your stuff went with someone else's when it was all in mint condition, so it is downright remortifying when you're one of the undead and you have to figure out what to do if a piece, or even an entire required part, has fallen off!

REMEMBER, EVERY BODY HAS THIS PROBLEM
It's one of those topics that is always on the minds of *both* zombies during a date. What if things go well—*really* well—and you go back to its place? There's always the chance that the parts that remain may not be up to snuff, and that can lead to frustration and heartache.

If you start feeling those carnal juices gurgling, it may be time to have "the talk." Don't approach it too early, but when you are all warmed up, be ready to talk about your (ahem) shortcomings.

HOW'S IT HANGING?
If you still have the proper equipment, check to be sure that it's still in working order. It's a tough and embarrassing question but one that needs to be asked regularly as you go through various stages of decomposition.

If you're intact, undamaged, and fully functioning, consider yourself one of the lucky ones! (But don't think it will last unless you take care.) If not, what's the issue? Do you have some deterioration going on, or has that wound from the chain saw attack given you problems you thought rigor mortis would have solved? Depending on the condition of the equipment, there are some things you can do to get them ready for action.

TOUCHING YOURSELF . . . UP

If the issues are purely cosmetic, e.g. suffering from a gangrenous hue that has discolored your goods, a topical touch-up should do the trick. Both Dutch Boy and Behr have a wide range of quality colors available to match your ethnicity and preference, and if you go with a weatherproof, outdoor paint, then you can ensure durability. You may need to do a light sanding first, followed by a coat of stain-killing primer before applying. Thank Zombie Jesus your ability to feel pain died with your first life!

If you find that your genitalia have experienced severe damage, you will have to take more aggressive steps to make them functional. If you've got anything left to work with, apply Bondo auto-body filler to the affected area, and sculpt the material to replicate (and maybe enhance, 'cuz why not?) your anatomy. Be sure to let the area dry before use, or you could really get stuck on each other!

IMPROVISE!

If you've got nothing left down there, you are actually lucky. You can get a better-than-your-own prosthetic from any adult store or online. With some latex, superglue, and a few AA batteries, your sex life will be more alive than ever!

And what if you fall apart during sex? And I don't mean emotionally. Guys, don't spoil the moment by crying over lost limb. Instead, impress your lover with innovation. You've probably got leftover parts lying around the den. Grab one that looks good and go with it! More on this to come.

Ladies, if you were hit with a shotgun blast while fleeing up a ladder, or some such incident, using your girly bits might be like throwing a hot dog down a hallway. Maybe that knife wound in your side is the better option now. The Vikings were partial to eye sockets. The only rule in undead sex is if it feels good, do it!

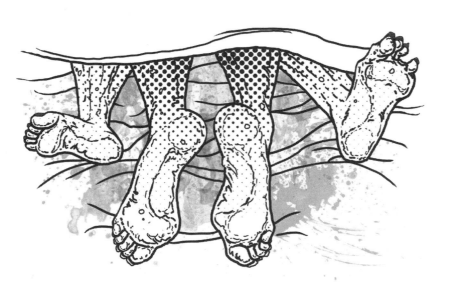

"I THINK THIS BELONGS TO YOU" AND OTHER AWKWARD CONVERSATIONS

As an undead, you are vulnerable to a lot more potentially embarrassing situations than the living. Organ sacks never have to worry about a sneeze that actually pops theirs eyes out of the socket or a cough that sends their tonsils sailing across the room. You are to be commended for your courage and the inhuman strength you muster to get through each day. It takes a great deal of guts (intact or otherwise) to crawl out of the pit each morning!

OH, THAT'S MY . . .

Limbs severely weakened by decay and organs riddled with fungus and parasites don't have the tensile strength they once did. That said, it is not uncommon for parts to wear or break off during a particularly vigorous session of lovemaking. Sometimes it's the arm that cracks under pressure, or sometimes it's something more vital that detaches. These are the things that can make for unpleasant conversations surrounding intimacy—and unfortunately sometimes during.

And what about when you find a butt cheek on your couch, an upper pallet in a coffee mug, or a finger stuck in your hair? Um, that wasn't yours, was it? You'll have to make a phone call that starts with, "I've got half your ass in my freezer. I think you can probably salvage it," though it makes even your pallid cheeks blush.

WHAT TO DO

If something like this does occur, decide if the lost part can be saved and if it's worth saving. If the answer is yes, make an immediate attempt to reattach it. (Yet another reason to keep duct tape and industrial staples close at hand.)

If you decide that it cannot be repaired or reattached with any degree of quality, then you need to dispose of it in either an incinerator or just bury it out back. Just make sure you bury it deep enough so that the neighborhood dogs and raccoons can't disinter it and parade it up and down the street. Awkward!

THE TALK

Once you've got that under control, you and your lover need to sit down and have an honest conversation about the events that have unfolded. Sure, you're both feeling bad about it. One of you is feeling *really* bad about it. But now is the time to see how strong your relationship truly is.

Start by gently taking its hand. GENTLY! Tell it you know it might be mortified, but you know this part of the afterlife. It's bound to happen to some part at some point in time. Now that the incident is over, you can move on, anticipating the day when you can both look back and laugh.

If the two of you can joke it out, then you have got a great shot at a long-term relationship based on humor, understanding, and mutual respect. You just made it through a traumatic experience, and the two of you came out feeling lighter in the end. Congratulations!

AND IF IT ALL GOES TO POT . . .

If things fall to pieces (sorry) because of some unfortunate accident, then the relationship wasn't that strong to begin with. This sort of thing is going to happen to both of you. Probably more than once. It's for the best that you find out sooner than later if something is a bad match or not cut out for dating in the afterlife. Don't feel bad; the afterlife is tough! Ultimately, you're better off with something that won't lose its head if you lose your nose.

PILLOW TALK

Ah, those postcoital chats! There you lay, comfortably spooning in a body bag on the tiled floor of a morgue. You've just shared a very meaningful moment, and now you're enveloped in bliss, accompanied by the soft sounds of your after-sex snack whimpering in anticipation.

TO SPEAK OR NOT TO SPEAK

As you stroke your lover's exposed shoulder blade, perhaps you want to mutter sweet nothings into its remaining ear. Or maybe you'd rather just listen to the stillness and quiet as the roaches and vermin explore your intertwined bodies in the cool night air.

If talking after makes you uncomfortable because your jaw came unhinged after all that action, but your lover really needs to share during this sensitive time, do you just let it chat as you nod and caress it dearly? What if you're the talker and your partner would prefer to just watch the mold grow? Either way, here are a few words of advice to help you through the chatter.

FOR THE SOILED AND SILENT TYPE

If you're not a talker, but your partner is, try to contribute at least a little—when it comes down to it, relationships are all about compromised decomposition. It'll be tough for you, but try to open up your rib cage and talk about the experience and how it made you feel. Let your lover know how special it is to you, even if you only take a few words to do it.

For example, after a long diatribe about how well your remaining parts fit together, all you have to do is look your partner square in its eye sockets, stroke its cheek flap, and say, "It's like you scraped the words right off my tongue."

Don't just yes it to death, though. Think of thoughtful ways to agree, and try to make contributions of your own. Little mutterings like, "You rot my world," or, "I wasn't truly reanimated until I met you," will win you tons of browning points.

FOR THE NIGHT-STALKER TALKER

The millipede-infested flour sack that serves as your pillow may be the place you might feel most comfortable to spill your guts, and that's OK. It's an intimate time and intimate talk certainly isn't out of line. There are some things you need to avoid discussing during these quiet times, though. The key is to keep it light, romantic, and avoid any topic that could possibly cause discord.

Never bring up past relationships, good or bad. Your mate will not appreciate hearing about what your ex particularly enjoyed or disapproved of. It is unwise to make comparisons to a previous lover, no matter how complimentary you think it may be. "Thank Satan that your butt has more meat on it than my ex's," is only going to make your partner think of you with another bony ass.

TURN IT AROUND

Whether you clam up or chit the chat after doing the dirty voodoo, there are some intimacy issues that you may feel you have to address if you're finding that the encounters aren't rocking your bones. Words of encouragement are always appreciated, as are compliments on a job well done. But if you have a complaint instead of praise, try to paint it in a positive light. Instead of "You just lie there like a stiff corpse," try "Your hard body is the best, and I'd love it if you ravaged me like you did that dog walker we had for dinner." This will make your partner feel good and let it know your needs without insulting or embarrassing it.

REGRETS: THE SHAMBLE OF SHAME

We've all taken that "shamble of shame." Creeping home after a night spent where it should not have been spent, waking up in the arms of something you're seeing in the full light of day for the first time. Embarrassing, yes, but you're not alone!

IT HAPPENS TO ALL OF US

It's one in the morning, and it's just you, the remains of the bartender who kept making bad Bloody Marys, and a flirty professional who's magically gotten more attractive over the course of the night. Since they unlive within walking distance of the bar, you agree to stagger it home.

Next thing you know, the sun is slowly warming the exposed patch of skull on your forehead and through the cobwebs and a wave of untreated sewage, you realize what is going on. You're hesitant to turn over and see what's next to you, but morbid curiosity and necessity require you to do so. Never have you seen such a horrific example of the innate cruelty of Mother Nature. Even for a zombie this one's bad—Carrot Top-in-the-sun-too-long bad.

THE DO'S AND DON'TS OF ESCAPE

You seriously consider tearing off your arm trapped under its pustulated neck to escape undetected, but you've only got that one left. You try to slide away quietly, but as you do its eyes open and a smile splits its unspeakable face.

Get up as quickly as you can, grab your clothes, make an excuse involving a sick relative who you've been meaning to have for dinner, and go. Fast.

Do give a fake e-mail. Don't give a fake number (they can call before you get far enough away). Do try to spare their feelings. Don't sacrifice your own (that will only hurt you both more later). Do get some hair of the dog in the hopes of forgetting your foul sins. Don't get it at the same bar, lest you repeat your mistake.

SO YOU'RE
A COUPLE NOW

CONGRATULATIONS ARE IN ORDER!

Through trial and error, disastrous dates, and gore-filled breakups with zombies who were all wrong for you—against all odds—you two intersected. You passed through the critical gauntlet of getting to know each other, braved stiff resistance from society and torch-wielding townspeople, and have finally found true love!

TOGETHER AT LAST

Now that you have something to share your undead existence with, you feel that the thing you call life has meaning again. You've merged your unlives and created a world wherein you can face the future together. With each other to count on, you'll be stronger, happier, and better prepared to run down those meals, face the angry villagers, and win on quiz night at the local bar.

You can share with them your hopes, aspirations, and midnight stalkings. No longer will you have to spend Friday nights on torturous blind dates arranged by your hapless coworker. Sunday mornings are no longer a dread, but a joy reading the *Times* in bed while your partner whips up a delicious breakfast of the neighbor you stole the paper from. Evenings can be spent cuddled up with *Deadwood* on DVD or enjoying a chuckle with another hilarious episode of *The Walking Dead*.

THROUGH GOOD AND BAD

You'll have something to lean on in tough times as well as good. When you have a hard night on the prowl, your partner will be there to offer a bony shoulder to cry on or hand you a filthy rag to wipe away your oozing tears. Barring any sniper fire, Molotov cocktail–tossing rednecks, or broadsword-wielding breathers, you two can plan on a long and happy afterlife together!

GETTING ALONG WITH ITS HORDE

When you're meeting its friends for the first time, you know you're being judged the second you walk through the door. They're measuring you up against your sweetmeat's exes and track record, but don't take it personally. You are the new non-person in their friend's afterlife, and they don't want to see their old chum get hurt.

BE ON YOUR BEST BEHAVIOR
This is no time to be the afterlife of the party. Stick with your partner and let it make the introductions. Don't be overly familiar with either the living or the undead. You need to remember that they are sitting in judgment of you.

It's a safe practice to think of this as a first date. Feel free to "talk shop" when it comes to your eating habits and offer up success stories, but be sure not to brag. Be complimentary, but don't pander. If someone is holding up well with the crowbar permanently lodged in their pelvis, comment on how handy it must be to have a weapon always at the ready, but don't overdo it.

Take interest in them, because even though you're the one being put through the paces, the best way to win something over is to ask it about itself. Whose corpse did they pull that awesome tie from? How has their luck been stalking down by the railroad depot lately? Little conversation starters like these break the ice and can help put all parties involved at ease.

IF THINGS GET AWKWARD
What if your date gets lost in conversation with an old friend, or someone forgot the pâté and it gets roped into going on a food run? Now you're in a room full of strangers, trying not to ooze through your shirt.

It's tempting to pull out your cell phone and start texting to look busy and popular. Fight this urge! Now is a rare chance to get to know your partner's friends zombie-to-zombie. You can ask how they know your mate, and maybe you'll find out something new! Don't confuse interest with digging for dirt and pry open any coffins that you weren't invited into. Just set up a topic, and let them roll with it. If they're good enough to be your partner's friends, who knows, maybe they'll one day make it into your inner circle, too!

IF ITS BEST FRIENDS ARE BREATHERS

Be extra attentive when you're being introduced to their living friends. They are naturally suspicious of you to begin with, and the fact that you have their friend's heart in your clawlike hands makes them even more so. Be deferential and nonthreatening without groveling.

Try to keep your usual, possibly off-putting habits and facial tics in check. It's not acceptable to stare hungrily at a voluptuous young lady or solid young man. No matter how delicious you're certain they taste, no drooling! Keep a tissue or handkerchief available to control any unwanted salivating. Yes, it IS a veritable banquet, but now is not the time. As long as you remain cool, collected, and ignore your rumbling gut, you stand a pretty good chance of getting out without incident. For extra insurance, eat before you go.

BE WARY

If any of the living seem to be overly anxious, most likely they are only tenuously associated with your date and are there out of some sort of obligation. Nervous and sometimes even hostile, these are the troublemakers. Avoid any conversations with them beyond civil niceties, and move on before they try to bait you into a fight with their rhetoric and tasty brains.

MEETING THE FAMILY

You thought meeting its friends was tough, but family members have an even greater distrust of new partners. They've raised and nurtured this person to become the boil or ghoul it is today, and here you are, wedging yourself into its soupy heart with sweet talk and sweetbreads. Naturally they are going to be more than a little suspicious of you and your intentions, so don't feel insulted. They'd be just as wary if you were all still alive.

BE PREPARED FOR EVERYTHING

No doubt your partner has prepared its family by warning them about any physical points of interest you may be sporting, imploring that they not stare or bring them up. But be prepared for questions about things you don't think they know about. Your darling has surely shared some stuff that goes beyond the superficial.

Though they've been pleaded with to be gracious, you'll be lucky to get some tight-lipped civility. The undead aren't really known for their manners and social skills, so if you are perceived as threatening or not good enough for their precious baby, things can go south fast. Stay nimble, and avoid fights at all costs. As the outsider, the best thing to do is duck their blows, both verbal and physical.

PLAY THE PART

You can control your behavior, clothes, and what goes in and comes out of your mouth. So think of this initial meeting as a job interview. Wear something nice but not flashy. Small stains are acceptable, but eat before you get dressed so you don't arrive slathered in your last meal.

Be polite, but don't gush. If you bring a gift, make sure it's something small, otherwise you'll look like you're trying to bribe them. A nice bottle of wine is appropriate if they drink, a galvanized bucket of small intestine if you're not sure.

IF/WHEN YOU SCREW UP

And if you slip up? Things that under most circumstances would be shrugged off or politely excused can seem like Hindenburg-level disasters when under the magnifying glass of something else's family. Accidentally leave an odorous stain on Aunt Mindy's antique settee? Innocently give a wino foot to Uncle Clive, who you didn't realize is now only stalking AA members? You'll never hear the end of it.

Regardless of how well you present yourself, you will be subjected to over-the-top scrutiny and have to handle it with grace. Be confident that your partner's opinion of you won't change with that of other people or people eaters.

REMEMBER THAT IT GETS EASIER

Once you've gotten past the first round of interrogations, things should start to go more smoothly. You can move beyond the "getting to know you" stage to ask about your partner's early years and feel more comfortable sharing entertaining rampage tales.

The goal is to make them as comfortable around you as their zombie offspring feels. Put them at ease with light banter. A tasteful joke or anecdote can go a long way toward building camaraderie. With perseverance, humor, and the ability to control your more base instincts, it won't be long before you, too, are calling its parents Mom and Dad.

HOW TO TREAT ITS CAPTIVES

When you come across a meal at your ghoulfriend's place, all wrapped up and ready to go, it's tempting to just dig in. Whether they're in a makeshift pen in the basement, in a steamer trunk bound with duct tape, or simply hog-tied and stashed under the sink, you'll be compelled to eat now, ask forgiveness later. This would be a huge faux pas, and you'll likely pay for that life with one of your limbs.

PATIENCE!

If you are at your date's cave and you happen to come across dinner before it's properly presented, consider a few things before chowing down.

Remember you're still a guest in this home, and you need to treat the pantry with the proper degree of restraint. While it's acceptable to make polite conversation over a captive's screams and pleas for help, it is not all right to rip off an ear for a quick snack simply because you didn't want to wait for the appetizers.

Avoid licking prisoners like a fat kid who can't help sticking his fingers in the icing of someone else's birthday cake. Try not to let your stare linger for too long over any exposed flesh. It makes captured breathers tense, and then they'll be less tender at mealtime.

HELP OUT

If you're left alone with a captive, and you need to break the uncomfortable silence before you break open its skull, ask it how it managed to get caught. Does it have any regrets or last words?

If you want to lend a hand with dinner, offer to give the meal a good scrub down or, even better, take the initiative by dragging it out back and putting it under the hose without being asked. It's a great way to demonstrate your thoughtfulness, and it's just plain fun!

INTER-LIVING DATING

Most once-unspoken societal rules of behavior have been broken over the past hundred years. Some of them have become the norm, like unmarried couples cohabiting, same-sex couples freely expressing their affections, or rampant use of the non-word "irregardless."

BREAKING SOCIETY'S LAST TABOO

These trends have somehow become acceptable, and yet zombies are still subjected to an unfair share of criticism, defamation, and gunfire. When you are one of the walking dead and spend most of your free time stalking, killing, and eating the living, you've already got a lot going against you. People tend to judge you harshly and use this lifestyle as evidence of your differences and "danger to children."

In addition to myriad social problems that revenants are forced to deal with every day, there still remains one major taboo that directly affects us to an inordinate degree: inter-living dating. After decades of progress in the field of zombie rights, a romantic coupling of the living and the reanimated is still treated like the pariah it was a hundred years ago.

LOOKING INTO THE FACE OF ADVERSITY

For those brave souls who want to make a go of it, dating can be extremely challenging. You'll be looked at with disgust, zombies and humans alike will snigger behind your back, and other flesh-bags will try to "save" your date from the flesh-eating monster they're with, i.e., you.

It can grow tiresome and terribly frustrating when you're repeatedly forced to explain to the ever-present horde of towns-folk and disapproving purist zombies that you're not hurting anyone—more so than usual, anyway. Like the love between a man and his Japanese body pillow, the love between a breather and someone who is life-challenged is rarely understood. Years of ignorance and fear have created an atmosphere of distrust, suspicion, and intolerance that affects us to this very day.

RIPPING OFF THE FACE OF ADVERSITY

The undead are making inroads into modern society. They are holding steady jobs, making contributions to the arts, and helping to thin out the homeless. But with all the progress and all the swearing that "some of my best friends are zombies," people usually change their tune if their breather son or daughter wants to date a member of the undead.

Small, vocal rallies in support of inter-living dating have begun to spring up in major cities, but they are usually out-shouted by the pro-lifers. A few high schools allow mixed dates to attend dances, but they are "special" dances set up for these "special" cases. And while some liberal churches have become accepting of these alternative relationships, none will perform an inter-living marriage, because they define matrimony as between two *people* who promise to honor each other as long as they both shall *live*.

PATIENCE IS A VIRTUE

These may seem like tainted victories, but bear in mind they are victories. Change takes time, and while patience is not the strongest suit for revenants, try to have some. If you are involved in an inter-living relationship, or support the right for all bodies to love how they wish, remember things will only get better if the world is constantly confronted with their fear made to live with it. So be public and proud to fight for the cause!

SO YOU LOVE A BREATHER

You've finally found that special someone, they're everything you could ever want in the whole universe, and . . . they're one of the living. It's better to admit up-front that this is not the easiest match to make work, so you can face any problems headlong instead of avoiding them like you do swimming and gun stores. The two of you have made a decision that will present countless obstacles for your happiness.

LUCKY FOR YOU, LOVE IS BLIND

You are to be commended for your courage and commitment to each other. You have managed to control your instinctual drive to feast on their warm, pink flesh and suck the marrow from their freshly snapped bones. For their part they were able to put aside their fear and natural revulsion to see you for the loving individual you are.

FROM DIFFERENT SIDES OF THE TRACKS

Up until now the two of you have been living in different worlds. You once spent your days and nights skulking about deserted alleys, rifling through the Dumpsters behind hospitals and crouching in the bushes along biking paths. Your partner comes from a world of coffee shops, appletinis, and gym memberships.

Your idea of a fine meal consists of twenty feet of small intestine unraveled from a disemboweled deliveryman while theirs sounds French and looks like that stuff you dig out of your belly button. You love sleeping in a cool ditch under the stars and a blanket of fallen leaves, but they insist on being mummy-wrapped in three-hundred–thread-count Egyptian cotton.

UNCOMMON GROUNDS

You've both made some major sacrifices for love. They've given up their dream of marrying a doctor or model and living in a condo on the thirtieth floor, while you've put aside your fantasies of going on a cross-country eating spree that ends in a violent standoff on historic Cannery Row. These concessions are proof that you two have a good shot at success.

To make it work, though, you're both going to have to do things that may be outside your comfort zones. You can't build a relationship solely in the safety of your hideout and the darkness of movie theaters—you'll have to go out in the world together, facing prejudice and doing things that make each other happy.

Joining them in a bowling league may not be the kind of alleys you prefer, but remember that you've got them accompanying you to the morgue for a potluck dinner this Friday with your friends. The truth of the matter is, you're going to find yourself in a lot of mixed company, so be prepared to endure the aroma of breathers who are off-limit snacks.

MAKING IT WORK—TOGETHER

You'll certainly find other things you have to adjust to over the course of your relationship. You might not be as fashion-conscience as your mate would like, and they are not as comfortable with the stench of decay as you are. You may prefer that they shut the door completely when using the bathroom, just as they would rather you not drag your most recent kill across the rug.

Whatever your differences and foibles, you have found each other in a great, big, indifferent world and have overcome near-insurmountable odds to be together. And that's the key to it: togetherness. You're going to face a lot of challenges out there—up next, telling your friends and family—and the only way it will even be worth working at is if you do it together. So don't go biting your partner's head off when the dry cleaning bill comes in, and hope they don't break out the sawed-off when they find your hair and scalp in the drain day after day.

WHEN FRIENDS AND FAMILY DON'T APPROVE

As the blissful couple you are, you've created your own routines and systems for how to work and play together. You've found you can do great things when you put your minds to it and have found success in all that you've attempted as a team. You've been made stronger by overcoming adversities that face a mixed-life couple. But now you face the ultimate challenge:
telling your friends and family.

BE COOL, BECAUSE THEY WON'T BE

In living-on-living relationships, the introduction of a new significant other can be a happy moment. This will not happen to you. You may have a couple of supportive people in your lives, but this meeting is going to go down like a freshman pledging a frat: awkward, loud, and eventually covered in vomit. Only after the snarls and yowling have subsided to a tolerable level (and any afflicted parties have been resuscitated) can you begin to discuss the situation as adults.

You need to maintain maximum coolness and level-headedness at all times. Let them know that while you love and respect them, you are an adult and can make your own decisions. You've looked for love elsewhere over the years, and ultimately this is where you have found the most happiness. Just as you are asking them for acceptance, you, in turn, need to be equally patient with them. A complex situation like this calls for understanding from all the parties involved.

ACCEPTANCE WON'T HAPPEN OVER NIGHT

There's a very good chance that until your friends and family actually get to know your mate, all they will see is a delicious meal going to waste while there are starving zombies out there. This may be technically true, and that's why you have to show them the qualities that make this person more than a meal—otherwise, why would you have fallen in love with them, right?

Tell them about your companion's good points, illustrating them with amusing anecdotes that are relatable to the undead, like how your love is an expert rat killer back at the hovel.

If you proceed slowly and with patience, it won't be long before your loved ones accept your partner. Who knows—in time your family might invite your special someone over for Thanksgiving without trying to convince you that you're bringing the main course!

MEETING THEIR FOLKS

No matter how controversial your relationship may be with your horde, they're your undead, and you know how to handle them—like making sure they eat before you show up with your partner. Meeting your main squeeze's family, on the other hand, is where the real challenge lies.

There's going to be a lot of yelling, tears, and cowering that happen every time you open your mouth. Or come over. Or get within their visual range. Or they hear your name. The only way they will get over their fears is if you don't feast on their tender flesh and delicious brains. They don't need to know about the incredible hunger you suppress every time the mouth-watering scent of their terror washes over you.

BE A LITTLE BIT TRICKY

To keep yourself in check, have a big meal before you go. Once there, pretend eating them is the furthest thing from your mind. In fact, you don't even like eating people that much. What your really enjoy is a nice rare steak or an assortment of sushi. These white lies will set them at ease and allow them to accept you for who are—mostly.

If they continue to make afterlife hard for you even though you've been nothing but polite time and time again, remember: You're a zombie, so eat their damn brains! You'll catch a lot of heat for it, but your honey knew what you are when the relationship started, so just plead undead.

DEALING WITH PREJUDICE

Prejudice is an ugly entity that rears its unwelcome head, affecting people from all walks of life. Sex, skin color, age, weight, height, ethnic origin—just about any descriptor can be the source of judgment by insecure jackasses who are so unsatisfied with their own lives that they are hell-bent on making everybody else suffer.

UNLIFE ISN'T FAIR

There are laws in place to protect people from these types of bigotries, but there are no safeguards for the undead. Zombies are unfairly subjected to verbal threats, dirty looks, and sniper fire. Too many times the undead are prey to cudgel-carrying mobs or gang-laden pickup trucks aiming for vehicular zombieslaughter.

There are more subtle forms of prejudice as well. Stiff smiles from maître d's accompanied by, "I'm sorry, but we're completely booked," "We're out of stock—try Walmart," muttered by snooty salesclerks, or worse, "Jesus, you're leaking all over the place! Get the hell out of this elevator!"

PROTECTING YOU AND YOURS

Mixed-life couples are especially vulnerable to prejudice. From the subtle slight by a hostess who refuses to seat you in an obviously empty restaurant, to a torch-toting mob of pro-lifers chasing you out of the county fair, you will face discrimination almost everywhere you go. This can lead to blood-spattered killing sprees, which may satisfy you, but they will be a turnoff for your breather.

The best thing you can do is support each other, be strong, and don't let idiots get between you. You will have to protect your fragile breather from physical attacks, while they will be better at dealing with mental ones because of that big, juicy brain of theirs. If you work together, no one can drive you apart.

MAKING IT THROUGH THE LONG HAUL

We can all get on each other's nerves at times. Even if one of you happens to be down to a meager brain stem and sinewy spinal cord flapping in the wind, something is bound to be irksome.

TELLTALE SIGNS OF AN IMPENDING RAGE EXPLOSION

Has a little chilly attitude or distance arisen between you two star-crossed lovers? You might be putting up a wall because it went rampaging without you, and you don't even realize you're doing it. If you've been taking the frontal lobe at dinner, even though it's your honey's favorite and you don't really care for it, you're acting out passive-aggressively, and that's not healthy!

Or maybe the cold draught is coming at you, and you have no idea what caused the crack that's letting it in. All you know is you woke up on a seemingly normal morning, and the light of your afterlife was shooting daggers at you through its remaining eye. It may even be giving you a silent-as-the-grave treatment when you try to chat it up over breakfast, only breaking the tension to gurgle, "Is that all you can say!?" before stomping off to its hidey-hole. Then you're left with your jaw on the floor, wondering what the hell just happened.

You need to figure out what is causing this little freeze pronto. After all, it's hard to make amends when one of you is not even sure what it is you did! Did it make plans for the weekend without asking you? Maybe you're sick of being criticized for how your skull-cracking technique leads to unnecessary hemorrhaging, but you don't care, because you like it juicy. Whatever happened needs to be fixed.

WHAT TO DO

You need to talk this out before the silent treatment becomes a habit. It doesn't take long for communication to go from little to zilch, and not because your vocal cords were just scraped. In a short time you'll each be off in separate, darkened corners of the hovel, noisily munching away on your piece of the day's catch and avoiding each other's eyes, then you'll go to bed without talking.

Before things get this far, sit down with your partner—preferably after feeding so you can both focus. Start by complimenting each other. Tell it how much you love the way its stench brings tears to your eyes. Spend some time reminding each other what first kindled your passion. On the journey, you'll likely find the bump in the road that's causing the problem, but in light of all the good stuff, it will seem like a mere burial mound instead of a mausoleum.

DON'T GO TO BED ANGRY

Couples who have been married for a long time share a common rule: Don't go to bed angry. It seems like a pretty simple axiom, but it's an invaluable one if you can follow it. Why is that? Because the more time you put between the argument and the resolution, the more difficult it will be to resolve the problem.

Try to look at your squabbles as you would the many gaping wounds that cover your bodies—if you attend to them in a timely manner with the right amount of staples, duct tape, and cosmetics, they won't be as bad as if you left them to fester. The sooner you kiss and make up, the better it will be for everyone.

Plus, nobody sleeps well when they're upset. Anger is a proven stressor to the body, alive or otherwise. It wears on whatever remaining blood pressure and circulation you may have and can keep you awake with guilt, frustration, and worry. Lack of zzz's quickly leads to loss of coordination, irritability, and reduced mental capacities—needless to say, you can't stand for much of that.

So talk it out, so you can once again sleep comfortably in whatever passes for each other's arms!

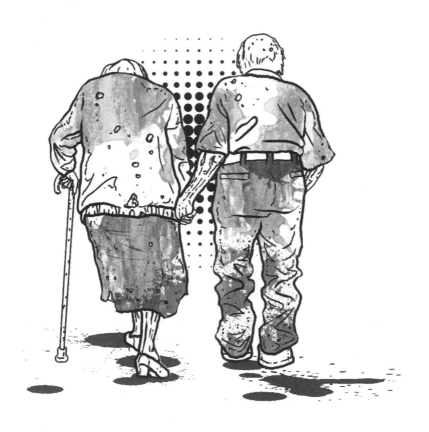

CARVING OUT SOME "YOU" TIME

Everyone requires some private time and a place to enjoy it. It's good to recharge and take a breather from the nonstop world of obligations, meetings, and running down prey that are sporting the newest cross-trainers. As work takes its toll, along with family, friends, and domestic issues, it's the cumulative strain that weighs down on even the strongest zombie, threatening to crumble your deteriorating bones.

Some deal with stress through meditation and exercise, others through regular visits to a therapist. These are healthy, positive ways to cope with the ups and downs of your daily existence, but they may not be enough. Sometimes you need to hunker down in a mud pit with a good book or stretch your limbs on a solo nature shamble to renew your energy and face another day at the rat race.

YOU BOTH NEED IT!

It is extremely important that you and your partner know and accept the fact that there are times you just shouldn't be around other beings. As confusing or hurtful as this may be at first, it's in everyone's best interest that you have a safe "getaway" spot.

Once you've come to the understanding that some "me" time is a necessity, then you can start to plan ahead, maybe even make it a regular scheduled break. Clearing one's head down by the abattoir or with a twenty-minute nap in the crawlspace is enough to recuperate and tackle life together with triple-strength and passion.

FINDING WHAT WORKS FOR *YOU*

It may take a while to figure out what sort of alone-time activities are the most restorative for you. You will have to reach down inside to find your center, which is much harder than reaching down into a fleshbag's center to find its spinal fluid. It helps if you have a quiet place in the house or shipping container that you can crawl off to and call yours—even a shallow indentation under a stack of palettes can do the trick!

Some prefer to experience their alone time in comfort, their pus-weeping head on an overstuffed pillow, earbuds dutifully inserted, and Kenny G filling their cranium with smooth jazz, whereas others are content with the warmth of the hollow behind the furnace accompanied by the sounds of a whimpering lunch lady shackled to a pipe. It's up to you to find that sweet spot where you're able to shed your troubles.

Going brain-dead in front of the TV might be a tempting outlet, but it's not ideal. You're not really alone when you're letting the idiocy of *World's Funniest Home Invasions* or *Decomposing with the Stars* into your thoughts.

ALONE MEANS ALL ALONE

Don't interrupt your other half's alone time. Unless villagers are knocking down the door with torches, you have to promise to leave each other be until you're both ready to emerge on your own. Trust is a very important aspect of this practice, and it must be maintained. If you do, soon you'll discover that you're both feeling fresher, better rested, and more at peace with yourselves and the world!

IF YOU DON'T . . .

Without a little time to unwind, you will likely find your outlet on a destructive path of alcohol and four-day-old roadkill. All-night benders that leave you covered in guts and gore and a horrifyingly tacky Hawaiian shirt are sure to quickly wear on your relationship. And when you consider the fact that you're doing it as a form of escape, you'll realize alone time is precisely that, minus all the bad choices and embarrassments.

ARE YOU THE JEALOUS TYPE?

A revenant approaches a hot zombie in a graveyard and asks, "You know, I've lost my girlfriend here in the cemetery. Can you talk to me for a couple of minutes?"

"Why?" she asks.

"Because every time I talk to a beautiful woman, my girlfriend appears out of nowhere."

A LITTLE IS PLENTY

It's true that a little bit of the green-eyed monster is fine—even welcome—in a relationship. It can keep you on your toes if you start to take your partner for granted, while at the same time bolstering your mate's ego. Everyone wants to feel appreciated, and a glint of jealousy in your lover's remaining milky eye can do that. Don't deny it!

If the two of you are out on the prowl and you attract the attention of some sexy, recently reanimated rottie, you're going to feel pretty darn good about yourself, even if your partner does get a little bent out of shape. The key word being "little."

KEEP IT IN CHECK, OR IT'LL DRIVE YOU APART

The problems arise when that glint turns into an emerald glow, and anger and resentment take root in you or your partner's festering heart. Jealousy can put unwarranted stress on your relationship, foster distrust, and eventually tear you apart like so much sweet, sweet cartilage.

If either of you feels that things are getting out of hand, address the issue before irreparable damage is done to your partnership. At first, the two of you should try to work things out on your own. Nobody has as intimate knowledge of the workings of the relationship as the two of you, so you have a good shot at solving the problem yourselves.

THE HEART OF THE PROBLEM

You love your partner, and it loves you. You know it, and it knows it, right? It has mouthed those three special words through withered lips into your worm-infested ears, and you've reciprocated with similar sentiments. So why the insecurity?

Jealousy is often an indicator of underlying issues caused by rotten baggage from past relationships, troubled childhood reanimations, and other incidences that have roots deep in the psychology of the undead and living alike.

If you find that you're unable to resolve the problem, then you may want to talk with a professional brain-shrinker. Those things lurking beneath the murky surface of consciousness may need some third-party coaxing to draw them out. There are many qualified counselors out there with the experience required to help you battle these tough issues, so you have no excuse to let things get even worse!

IS JEALOUSY AN ISSUE WITH YOU TWO?

TAKE THE QUIZ!
Backbiting can deteriorate a relationship faster than an unembalmed corpse in an unmarked grave. Do you think your play-jealousy might boil over into rage-jealousy? Best to figure out what boils your secretions before the gangreen-eyed monster blinds your love, and you end up hacking up the relationship.

YES OR NO?
1. I get irritated when my mate gets attention from others.
2. I'm starting to view everyone with suspicion.
3. I devoured the mailman for saying "good morning" to my partner.
4. I think the cashier at the supermarket is making inappropriate comments to my significant other.
5. That cashier was delicious.
6. Sometimes I think my partner's rags are too low-cut.
7. I hate when my partner talks to strangers of the opposite sex.
8. It bothers me when my mate eats people of the opposite sex.
9. It concerns me when my partner takes calls into the other room.
10. I've attempted to read its e-mails.
11. I'm resentful of its opposite-sex coworkers.
12. I've considered eating its opposite-sex coworkers.
13. I've opened my lover's mail and/or packages.
14. I've opened the chest cavities of people who smiled at it.
15. I may have overreacted in some cases.

If you answered *yes* to three or more of these questions, then you may have a serious issue with jealousy. Definitely talk to your partner about your feelings, and consider getting professional help if your covetous rages start to take a toll on the relationship.

DON'T PLAY THE "BLAME GAME"

As you are well aware, honesty is the best relationship policy. Whether it be with your partner, a family member, or your embalmer, the need for a truthful dialogue cannot be overemphasized. When something is troubling you, be mature and don't resort to pettiness and groaning about it. There's not a lot you can do to control how your partner is going to react to relationship issues, but there are a few things you can do to make a conversation about them go more smoothly.

THE DO'S
Make sure you pick a good time to talk. If it just came back from a terrible shamble, where all it could catch was a skin-and-bones granny, now is not the time. Conversely, if it just came back from the best hunt of its afterlife, don't spoil its moment. Instead, pick a time where you are both feeling relaxed and well fed.

Speak openly and honestly about your feelings, even if they're not exactly what your partner wants to hear. Don't hold back. If it expects you to do all the housework after it traipses in mud and guts, don't just ignore your anger—tell your mate you are feeling walked all over and that you want to share the scum bucket chores.

Let it make its own apologies and amends. It'll probably have enough feelings of guilt without you piling it on. If you lay off, it will respond better and be more apt to work with you on resolving the issue at hand. You'll be a better zombie for it, and it'll walk away with its pride intact.

THE DON'TS

Don't assign blame, even though you feel like you couldn't be more right and it more wrong. Unless it's trying to hurt you on purpose, then it is probably coming at things from a perspective you haven't considered. If you play the blame game, you'll put it on the defensive, and there are few things more dangerous than a cornered zombie.

Don't attack your mate, verbally or physically. It's counterproductive and will become a full-blown, no-holds-barred brouhaha with shredded skin, lank hair, and stained teeth flying everywhere. Keep an even keel, and don't point finger stumps.

Don't bring up any past arguments. Pulling old failings out at your convenience is playing extremely dirty. Do you want it to bring up your gore-soaked dalliance with that geriatric greeter from your local Walmart? Or how about that time you came home covered in more than glitter from a friend's bachelor party?

THE IT DEPENDS

If the problems were jointly caused, then the two of you need to work as a team to fix them. You'll find that issues created together may be easier to address than ones created by a single party. It takes the full weight of guilt off one zombie and spreads it out for a more balanced load.

Be it financial woes or the fact that you two devoured the ne'er-do-well son of a prominent politician and are feeling the heat in the form of harassment by local cops, you're in this together. No matter what happened or what's at fault, if you work bony hand in moldering claw, to correct the issue, you'll strengthen the relationship as you solve the problem.

THE ART OF GROANING "I'M SORRY"

Everyone messes up. Knocking over a cup of tea while reaching for a box of Cerebellum O's is easy to apologize for and mean it. "Whoops, I've got butterfinger-bones!" It's no sweat.

Then why is it so hard to say sorry for the big mistakes? Because no one wants to face their true failings. Sometimes it's hard to get those two simple words to form on your blistered tongue, but avoidance ulcerates a mistake into a bigger, sorer wound.

SWALLOWING YOUR PRIDE

It may taste bitterer than week-old stomach acid, but sometimes you have to swallow that pride. You done screwed up, and now you've got to own up. Whether you forgot your love's rebirthday, ran over Zombie Rover, or ate that tasty little number from town who you were forbidden from stalking, it's time to pay the price.

Saying you're sorry before you get caught will win you bonus points for honesty and bravery. Your partner isn't going to be happy; in fact it is probably going to be pissed off enough to make you sleep on the slab in the living room for a week, but it's better than the unbridled rage explosion you would face if you were caught blood-handed.

WORDS PROBABLY AREN'T ENOUGH

If this is one of those big screwups—and as a reanimated flesh muncher, you've done some *bad* things—then just groaning "I'm sorry" and looking ashamed is probably not enough. You're going to have to make several impassioned speeches, buy more than one grave blanket, and probably suffer through a minor wrong-doing on your partner's part as they try to make you suffer some comeuppance. All you can do is take it!

BREAKING UP WITHOUT GETTING BEATEN DOWN

There will come a time in your afterlife when you are presented with the realization that you do not love the thing you're with.

REALIZING IT'S NOT WORKING

It all started out so sweetly. Remember that Labor Day parade when you found yourselves tugging at opposite ends of a majorette behind the hardware store? Well, that instant attraction with the potential to blossom into something more has faded. Even if there was a time when you thought that this could be "the one" and images of your future together swirled through your parasite-infested mind.

But as time tore inky pages off the calendar, you began to find your feelings were not frothing into something beyond the initial attraction. "Give it some time," you said to yourself, "I'll get out of this emotionless funk soon." But eventually you discovered that something never clicked.

HOW TO SAY "I DON'T LOVE YOU"

Once you are consigned to the fact that the stars are not aligned, you will start wondering how you're going to get out of this dead-end relationship. You don't want to break the remains of your ghoulfriend's heart, but you know you can't keep pretending things are OK.

You look for outs, hoping to find something that would make it completely understand why you're dumping it without hurting its feelings and sending it into a limb-detaching rage. You pray it finds a job in another country, or, better yet, it starts an affair so you can call it quits and still be the better zombie.

But odds are that perfect excuse is never going to come. You're going to have to pull the trigger on the relationship, like a hillbilly with a double-barrel protecting his sister-cousin. But there's a right way and a wrong way to break up with someone.

THE RIGHT WAY

You will need to use every ounce of empathy, honesty, and respect you've got. It's going to be hurt that you're dumping it, and the longer you've been together, the more painful it's going to be.

Remember to be gentle and understanding. It will be emotionally fragile, feeling hurt and betrayed. There's a good chance it will lash out at you with accusations, flailing limbs, and gnashing teeth. Don't buy into it, and don't escalate the confrontation. Try to talk it down without being condescending or getting beat over the head with your own arm.

Be sensitive but firm. Don't feel guilty and fall back into an unfulfilling relationship. Resist the temptation for one more shamble through the back alleys or a "meaningless" night of breakup sex. Giving into these things will only make a bigger mess of an already wretched situation. Instead, give your now ex-partner closure. Let it scream at you until its jaw falls off, if that what it takes. Get it all out there, so you don't have to keep digging up old graves.

THE WRONG WAY

The wrong way is brusquely. It's tempting to send an e-mail or a text message, because you think short and sweet will be better than long and bitter, but you owe it more than that. You need to grow a pair—even if you've lost them in the literal sense—and have a shriveled-heart-to-dangling-cardiac-chamber.

Never do it in public, especially in a place that holds some emotional meaning, like a favorite date spot. You may think you can avoid a dramatic blowout this way, but you're likely to find yourself trying to use a Starbrains cup to protect your eyes from being clawed out by the angriest zombie you've ever seen as baristas and teenagers snicker at you.

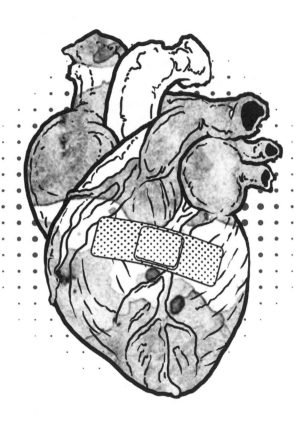

RECOVERING FROM A DUMPING

You've just been dumped by the only reanimated corpse that could ever make you happy in this miserable post-life existence that's filled with nothing but brains and guts and heartache. You were supposed to face the machete-wielding breathers together, endure the endless eons of unremitting hunger together, be the things that go bump in the night together. But your paramorgue left you, and now you're just a pathetic wad of rotting sinews that is all alone in a big, scary world.

TIME HEALS EVEN THE MOST PUTRID WOUNDS

That's just crazy! It's just your broken heart talking. It is a lot harder to heal a metaphorically broken heart than duct tape a physical one back together. No one is going to be able to gurgle some magical words to make you feel better, and reading this isn't going to miraculously pull you out of the dumps. It's going to take time to climb out of your pit of despair, but it *will* happen.

It may takes days, weeks, or even months, but at some point you're going to feel like your old self—not your old living self, but still good. You're going to remember there are other corpses rising from the grave every day, and you're going to crack your bony mandibles into a smile once more.

GET UNDER SOME BODY TO GET OVER SOME BODY

The rebound. It's the oldest trick in the book. Some will tell you it's not a good idea, but think of it this way: It is going to take you two shuffles forward, and then it's almost guaranteed to take you one stumble back. But that's still progress!

Just make sure you bounce back into the game with some body who is not likely to get hurt. You don't want to lay the same heartbreak that you're recovering from on some poor, lovesick night stalker—you've got enough bad karma already. And remember, stalker is part of the zombie nature, so keep that in mind when choosing your Mr. or Ms. Tonight.

HAPPILY EVER AFTERLIFE

CONGRATULATIONS!

You've finally found the one being you want to spend the remainder of your shambling, croaking existence with. Through trial and error, success and failure, you've found the light at the end of crypt. This is the creature whom you'll go into stasis with after feeding and emerge with when the moon is alighting on your moldering faces.

You're no longer wading through the bile-filled swamps of loneliness and spending many a hungry night curled up under a receiving dock in search of another flesheater who's into Civil War reenactments as much as you are. Just the thought of a crimson-soaked future with your post-soul mate makes whatever remains of your central nervous system go all atingle with misfiring synapses.

CHANGE IS GOOD!

You've gone through some major afterlife changes that have made you a happier, more fulfilled zombie. You now have the support and heart (possibly literally) of another, and you're about to embark on a wonderful, gut-munching adventure together. What more could you ask for?

Get ready to combine everything you've got. Your stuff, your hideout, your families, and more—it's all going to be legally its as well as yours. This may sound scarier than a deserted island with no breathers and no shade, but it's actually a good thing. You'll fill in each other's gaps (again, possibly literally, and this time in more ways than one), they'll be chipping in when you're tapped out, and you'll quickly realize that instead of having twice the stuff to worry about, it's really the same amount of stuff as when you were single, but now you've got two bodies taking care of it all.

WEDDING BELLS

By now you think that this is the one for you, but how do you know for sure if the bell tolls for thee?

YOU'VE NEVER BEEN HAPPIER, EVEN IN LIFE
Now this is true love! Even if you were married pre-reanimation, you can't remember being this content. Granted, that may be due to diminished mental capacity and brain loss. But still, every night feels like a vacation. One long, happy walk on a moonlit beach filled with glistening entrails. You feel like the ghoulish counterparts to Gatsby and Daisy, gaily spending your time in bloodied seersucker and linen, sporting boaters and parasols on fog-shrouded estates.

YOU SHARE EVERYTHING
They know you carry your stress in your shoulders (and your left shoulder in a bowling ball bag), and are always there to offer up a quick massage. You can pick up on the most subtle nuances in each other's behavior and can instantly tell if the other is having fun, hungry, ready to go, hungry, feeling down, feeling hungry, feeling hangry, or out-and-out starving.

You have found out everything there is to know about each other. You agree with the opinions and beliefs it holds, or you're at least able to stomach them. You know its favorite color (Pancreas pink, or PMS 176) and the body part it deems the most delicious (the hypothalamus). You are even OK with the fact that it bites its toenails and asks you to pop the boils on its back. If that ain't love, what is?!

BUT IF FEARS LINGERS . . .
Now that you are certain of your feelings for your partner, you want to pop the big question! But an inkling of doubt might still be present if you are not certain that it'll say yes. Do not give

into the fear! If you can face napalm plumes just to get a good brunch, you can do this.

If you don't act fast enough, your partner may get tired of waiting for a commitment, or they may start to believe you're not sure about the relationship, and move on. Don't risk losing this precious zombie. There are few chances at true love in anyone's life and even fewer in the afterlife. If you believe that you've found *the* one, then you have to make your move.

THE PROPOSAL

Where you propose should be exceptional. Consider a place that has special meaning to you both, like that spot along the river where you ambushed another young couple and jokingly referred to it as a double date while relishing each morsel of their once-enamored flesh. Maybe it's on a romantic vacation to the amply-stocked buffet that is Hong Kong or while visiting the charming Sedlec Ossuary in the Czech Republic. Wherever it is, it'll be perfect.

You can never be too romantic when you propose. You can stick with a tried-and-true gesture that has worked for generations and get down on one knee (assuming you have one to spare). It's cliché, but it's also a proven winner!

Maybe an alternate take might be more your style. A ring hidden in the brain stem of an imported Frenchman, a proposal spelled out in entrails on a secluded beach, or even a billboard on their shamble home from work would make for a truly memorable moment.

Treat the event with the sincerity it deserves. Don't get caught up in conventions unless you identify with them. Do things your way, and you're sure to get the answer you deserve.

YOUR ENGAGEMENT

OMZ! The proposal worked! Now it's time to move on to the next stage: the engagement.

WHO TO TELL FIRST

After you've come far enough down from cloud strychnine to remember the rest of the world still exists, you should tell everyone about your happy union. Don't hurt any of your loved undeads' non-feelings by making them feel left out in the announcement order. If your sister finds out after your old roommate, you're going to be in deep viscera.

Thanks to technology, you can avoid playing favorites. A quick picture e-message of you and your new fiancé works perfectly. You may still have to call your parents, though, as they probably still regard their cell phones with distasteful bewilderment.

THEN THE QUESTIONS START

Expect to be bombarded with questions by everyone you tell. Practical Mom will ask, "Have you set a date?" Your jealous, obnoxious roommate from the mausoleum will ask, "Are you pregnant?" And fat Uncle Sal will want to know, "What are you serving at the reception?"

Everybody will have questions, but you don't have to have all the answers yet. You may not know yet if you'll buy a house or rent after the wedding. And no, you don't know if you'll make children right away. While you certainly don't owe anybody any answers (after all, it's your engagement, not theirs!), remember they are (mostly) excited for you. So be gracious and keep your temper, even when your relatives are being tactless.

SAVE THE DATE!

Unless you've agreed to an open-ended engagement, decide on a date sooner rather than later. Are you basing it around any religious holidays or festivities? What about an anniversary? Remember, winter weddings are cheaper—and smell better.

Once you've made your decision, you can send out your save-the-dates. By this time, the whole thing will start feeling very real. But don't let your moldy bones begin snapping under the pressure, because now your energy has to go into fleshing out the details of your big day.

THE ENGAGEMENT PARTY

Ritual calls for the bride's family to throw the engagement party. Nowadays this event is up for grabs. The bride's horde can host the celebration at an all-you-can-catch restaurant, or the groom's family may have it at a park when a concert is happening so they don't have to spring for the food. Even you—the happy couple—may decide to throw a shindig at your shack.

No matter where it is hosted or by what, be prepared to rake in the booty, because the gifts will pour in! Try not to tear through them like a kid on Antichristmas morning, though, because then the thank-you cards will be almost impossible to write out. Did Aunt Hilda give you that thespian, or was it your friend Hector? Where did that kindergartner come from? You don't want to have to write a generic "Thank you for your generous gift" on all your cards, because everybody knows that means you have no idea who gave you what.

PLANNING YOUR SPECIAL DAY

There are countless details to figure out while organizing a wedding. From the type of ceremony down to whether or not you want chair covers (recommended for obvious reasons), you're going to be confronted with an astounding amount of options and decisions. Don't panic! Tons of undead do this all the time, and there are hordes of professionals who are hungry to help you. Just take things one step at a time.

THE VENUE

If your pickled hearts are set on a venue for the reception, inquire about their undead policy. The manager will most likely avoid scheduling any other parties for that day, as the possibility of dozens of inebriated flesheaters lurching about the hall and grounds, intermingling with the living from other parties, will only raise his already sky-high insurance premiums.

A number of undead-oriented venues have been springing up across the country. These places are fantastic for understanding your needs and tastes, offering options like a moonless evening spent desecrating graves and eating corpses. This will be a memorable hit of the wedding season for revenants, but it is likely to make any breathers you invite uncomfortable. Though they may be accepting of the undead lifestyle, being in the middle of by-zombie, for-zombie party will scare the intestinal stuffing out of even the most die-hard humbie.

BIG OR SMALL AFFAIR?

The size of your wedding can be a hard decision. You're on an emotional high right now and want to invite everyone from your sixteenth cousin to that homeless guy who disposes of your picked-over leftovers, no questions asked.

If you have a large family and want them all to share in the day's joy, consider if you can afford it. Unless you are independently wealthy or have rich parents, finances will play a big part in your final choice. You may have to sacrifice the filet amygdala entrée for a simple innards buffet if you want to invite your entire horde.

If you're limited on budget or have just decided to keep it small, then you have even more opportunities to do something unique. Imagine being able to hold your union in the embalming room of your favorite mausoleum. The Bianco Antico marble floors and walls, the brass fixtures, the amazing atmosphere—what more could you ever ask for?

THE CEREMONY

Weddings are often religious unions. If you decide to engage in one, speak with the cleric or mambo asogwe of your choice and reserve them for the date. You may have to attend some pre-marriage counseling, depending on the mandates of your chosen faith. These are typically easy sessions with the only challenge being not eating your holy person of choice before you get to your wedding day.

THE MUSIC

Instead of a DJ listlessly cranking out "Electric Slide" and "The Chicken Dance" for your guests, why not a sweet string trio or single harpyist playing the classics. If room permits, you can always go with a simple pianist taking requests all night. You won't see your Aunt Clara out there shaking it to Sir Mix-A-Lot, but you'll have the perfect musical accompaniment to a lovely and understated evening.

WEDDING CHECKLIST

- ○ Bride: Something old, something new, something borrowed, someone blue.
- ○ Groom: Tuxedo. Nerve (not nerves).
- ○ Maid of Horror: Make sure none of the undead maids eat any of the breather maids.
- ○ Flower Girl: Knows the aisle is no place to pick her nose.
- ○ Best Man-Type Creature: See Maid of Horror. You may actually want to keep them separated until the last minute.
- ○ Rings: Be sure you remove the previous owners' fingers before you slip them on your bony mate's.
- ○ Ring Bearer: Has the rings, knows they're not toys.
- ○ Ushers: Well-fed so they can exercise a modicum of self-control.
- ○ Bride's Parents: Have their checks cleared? Because the manager of the banquet hall isn't letting you in if they haven't.
- ○ Groom's Parents: Don't let them eat the bride's parents.
- ○ Organist or Pianist: You said pianist.
- ○ Readers: Know their parts. A passage from Psalms is always nice. Try to avoid the Book of Revelation.
- ○ Flowers: Something with a strong odor to mask the stench emanating from the wedding party.
- ○ Bridal Party Gifts: Jewelry for the bridesmaids, watches for the groomsmen.
- ○ Guest Book & Pen: You need to know where to send the thank-you notes, right?
- ○ Clergy: They make a fine sacramental snack on the way to the reception.
- ○ Aisle Runner: A good tarp should protect the carpeting from any stains, splatters, or spills.
- ○ Unity Candle/Candles: Be careful. *Very* careful.

THE HONEYMOON

Whether you're planning a relaxed romantic getaway in Cabo or something adventurous like big-game hunting in the Mid-west, you need to take into account a destination's climate, both weather-wise and politically. You don't want to end up at a place where you'll burn in the sun by day and burn at the stake by night.

Figure out if you are going to be greeted at the airport terminal with smiles and open arms or if you will be rushed off to a razor-wire–enclosed secret site by a platoon of soldiers in hazmat suits wielding assault rifles. Otherwise your happily ever afterlife will be pretty short-lived.

HONEYMOON HOT SPOTS AND HELL MOUTHS

Some eastern European countries are very accepting of the undead and offer great foggy, mountainous landscapes for you and your new spouse to stagger through, dining on succulent, locally fed villagers and violating some of the world's oldest crypts. Most American and Canadian destinations are considered zombie-friendly due to the popularity of "reality"-based television and their plethora of alternative lifestyle shows.

Japan and a few of the Pacific-Rim countries, on the other hand, have very low tolerance for the uninterred. Some Middle Eastern countries can also be a bit dicey. While they have accepted the flesheating habits of reanimated corpses, they still have issues with women. Ladies should exercise caution, keep covered, and not attempt to drive a car.

WHAT'S THE WEATHER LIKE?

While a camping honeymoon in the Sonoran Desert seems like a lovely way to spend your first two weeks as a married couple, the temperature rises to well over one hundred degrees in the afternoon. No matter how well-preserved you think you are, your tissues will not withstand that heat for an extended period. Even the highest SPF sunscreen, the darkest UV-blocking sunglasses, and the widest-brim hat cannot save you from the decomposing effects of the extreme heat.

If you enjoy the expansive vistas and beautiful palette of the desert, then perhaps consider a by-night honeymoon. Stay at your air-conditioned hotel in the desert by day, and go on hand-in-hand shuffles by night after the temperature drops from sweltering to shivering.

Climes of the opposite extreme, like the famous seasonal Ice Hotel in Norway, may sound unique and more palatable, but you're essential cold-blooded now, so your corpus is likely to freeze and become immobile fast! That's not the kind of stiff you want to be on your honeymoon.

WHAT TO EXPECT

Expect to have an amazing time! You probably have been in such a tizzy planning your wedding that you've practically forgotten what it's all for. Remember why you got married in the first place: Because you love being with each other so much that you wanted to make your ever-after real. Now you can return to those two things you do best: feeding and fooling around!

Get ready for the people at the hotel to call you Mr. and Mrs. Zombie. And expect a marathon of lovemaking, so have on hand lots of duct tape, glue, latex, lingerie, and whatever else you need to hold it together *and* get off. Know that this is a once-in-an-afterlifetime event, and no matter how slowly you try to shamble through it and savor every last cowering bellhop, it's going to fly by in a terrified fleshbag's heartbeat.

MAKING A HOVEL A HOME

Moving in together is a big step (and you can read this section even if you're deciding to live in unmarried sin)! You'll be combining the best of both of your nests into one new household. If you've never cohabitated with someone before, you'll find that it can be as rewarding as it is challenging.

YOUR PLACE OR THEIRS (OR NEITHER)?

The shallow pit you've hollowed out for yourself beneath the abandoned granary was fine before, but will it accommodate the two of you? Their supply storage in the doorless refrigerator dumped in the ravine was groovy, but is it spacious enough for you to keep both of your expansive wardrobes? If the answer is yes, then moving in together may mean moving into one of your hideouts.

But if you find that neither of your hovels is suitable for both your needs, you may need to dig around for another place. Settle on things you both want and need, like an on-site washer and dryer, lurching distance to a mall, and central air. Take your time finding a place you both agree on, because you're going in for the long haul and don't want a lot of groaning later.

TOO MUCH STUFF

By combining your possessions, you're bound to have more stuff than you need. You don't need multiple blenders or three sausage grinders! Carefully assess what the two of you have duplicates of, and keep the stuff in the best shape. In no time you'll have culled the redundant items from your inventory.

Moving is deadly expensive, so selling items on zBay or Dregslist is a great way to lop off the excess and make some green for the move in the process. There are limitations to what you are allowed to sell on these sites, so be sure to check their rules regarding the sale and transport of biological waste and bodily fluids.

GRAVEYARD SALE

Alternatively, you may want to host a graveyard sale. It's a big undertaking to select and individually price everything, but you don't have to go through the hassle of shipping things, and you get it all taken care of in just one day. Place ads in some of the local papers and tack up signs in the week leading up to the date to make sure everyone has had a chance to learn about it. You'll get a lot more money for items if you take the time to polish your wares and spot clean any stains. Febreze works wonders for covering up any lingering smell of death and decay!

WARMING UP YOUR NEW HOME

It's a good idea to purchase some new items together to make them "ours." Is your fifty-gallon drum rusting out after years of faithful service? Buy one of the new high-density polyethylene drums together! The two of you can be assured that your fermenting leftovers are secured and available for a snack, any time, day or night.

If you've been thinking about some new thumb cuffs or ball gags but have yet to commit to anything, why not pick something out together? Not only can you share the price, but imagine how exciting and meaningful it will be when you use them on that first "guest" you drag back to the house.

Once you pair down the excess junk to a manageable level and add a few new pieces, you will have turned a condemned apartment into your very own little pestilent home!

MINE VS. ITS VS. OURS

Blending two sensibilities can be confusing. Everything from the basics, like home décor or which car gets the garage, to less tangible things, like personal space and privacy, are open for debate. And though you love and respect each other, you may find yourself baring your teeth while your partner snarls at you that a Jackson Pockmark reproduction isn't art.

GIVING, TAKING, SHARING

You and your afterlove should discuss your cohabitation beyond who gets what side of the slab. Do either of you need an area in the home for a little "me" time? Even if all you need is a shallow grave under the porch, you need to bring it up.

Talk about what's considered private and what's open game for everyone to see. Opening mail might be okay, where as old photos may be off-limits. If you leave out pictures of your ex doing body shots off a half-eaten Jehovah's Witness, that's sure to unleash a rash of terror in the hood.

What about ownership of hygiene products? While you'll probably be sharing the basics like toothpaste and duct tape, how would you feel if they used your wire bristle brush for their own grooming and maintenance? These are things that can be addressed openly in the beginning so they don't turn into problems later.

IF THE PLACE ISN'T NEW TO BOTH OF YOU

If you're moving into their little cabin in the woods, it may have seemed comfortable before, but there could be some growing pains as you adjust to life together.

Be patient. Be flexible. There are few things that are worth warring over, so choose your battles wisely! While you may feel strongly that glassware be kept over the sink and bone saws next to the stove, is it really worth fighting about? *Really?* And though you may be used to only opening a new jar of jellied organs when one is finished, your partner may prefer to have a variety of flavors available. Again, is it worth raising the dead with your screeches over this?

DECORATING IS A TEAM SPORT

Once you've managed to work out the practical issues, you'll be able to sit back and focus on the aesthetics of your new hovel. This should be the fun part!

You may have to combine your taste on furniture. If your preference is for the clean, understated lines of Mission Style, but it prefers the colorful Memphis style from the early '90s, you'll have to compromise. It will take some work, but you can pick pieces from each style that complement each other, or you can divide up the rooms so you can each do your thing.

Pick up a few design magazines and watch *Beetlejuice* again, and see if anything catches your milky eyes. Even with your preconceived notions of what you do or don't like, your research will help you land on a common design ground.

SOMETIMES YOU JUST HAVE TO SAY OKAY

Of course, everyone has a few select items in their history that they carry with them no matter how many times they move. It could be a family photo album, a unicorn music box, or the pelvic girdle from their very first victim. No matter what it is, make an allowance for it and show that you appreciate how important the item is to your spouse—even if it makes you want to wretch.

FINAL FINANCES

Statistically, the issue of finances is the greatest contributor to marital discord. Money management is not a particularly pleasant subject when things are going well, and it can get nasty when there are rocks on the marital highway.

A PREEMPTIVE STRIKE

You can prevent issues from becoming hairy by recognizing the signs of a problem early. Consider your shopping habits and if your partner has an expensive hobby. Have you had financial problems in the past, perhaps even pre-reanimation? New laws are being passed all the time to try to collect debt revenants accrued while still alive. It is time for full disclosure with your partner, before the bounty hunters start showing up.

The best thing to do is set up a common household budget. Make sure the important bills (duct tape supply, rent/mortgage, utilities, embalmers) get paid before anything else. Next, what should be put into savings for a rainy day, followed by the budget for entertainment (movies, a glass human tank, etc.).

ANOTHER SOLUTION

Of course money problems are nonexistent if you decide to go "off the grid." While this was practically the only way for the undead to exist for a long time, in modern days most are either unwilling or unable to unlive in this fashion. We have jobs, friends, and family ties that keep us in the system.

But if this unusual yet fulfilling route appeals to you, you can find yourself an abandoned grain silo or summer camp to call home. No rent, no utilities, no taxes—just you, your spouse, and however many lost hikers you can poach.

REALLY? A BABY? YOU'LL ONLY EAT IT.

TAKE THE QUIZ!

Is anyone ever *really* ready for a baby? They are darling little afterlife-changers and tempting butterball snacks all rolled into one. If you feel the parental clock ticking in your otherwise dead man's chest, then maybe you have the self-control it takes to rear a child without devouring its sweet, juicy, ooey-gooey, good-ness. (Note: If the mere description of the quiz has made you hungry, you already have your answer.)

1. Have you always wanted a baby?

2. Have you always thought you'd make a good parent?

3. Do you get a special feeling in that space where your heart used to be when you see or hear a baby?

4. Do you get that special feeling in your stomach when you see or hear a wee one?

5. Do you find babies cute enough to just gobble up?

6. In your opinion, could every baby stand to fatten up a bit?

7. Have you ever licked food off a baby's face?

8. If so, did the baby taste better than the food?

9. Do you think you can handle the unpredictable hours those first few months?

10. Will your work schedule allow you the time needed to care for a baby?

11. Are you willing to bone up on an infant's unique dietary needs?

12. Do the cries of a hungry baby make you hungry as well?

13. Do you feel exhilarated when you see an infant take its first few steps?

14. Do you ever see a baby take its first few steps and think, *I could catch that thing without even trying?*

15. Have you ever nibbled on a baby's toes and then had trouble stopping?

16. Does that newborn smell make your mouth water?

17. Have you ever changed a diaper?

18. Have you ever given a baby a bath?

19. Have you ever given a baby a bath in a stainless steel stew pot instead of a li'l tub?

20. Do you believe in a gender-specific palette for your infant's nursery?

21. Do you consider Francisco Goya's *Saturn Devouring His Son* an appropriate theme for the nursery?

22. Do you know the classic bedtime storybooks?

23. Is Jonathan Swift's *A Modest Proposal* one of your favorite parenting guides?

24. Do you consider early enrollment in a prestigious preschool of paramount importance?

25. Do you consider it appropriate to allow a nanny to raise your child when you reenter the workforce?

26. If you discover the nanny failed to sterilize a bottle, is it appropriate to bite off their head?

27. Are you willing to arrange playdates for your child and their friends when they're older?

28. Will you be able to refrain from eating one or more of your child's more plump friends and/or their rotund parents?

If you answered *yes* to the following questions, congratulations! You are well on your way to mommy- or daddyhood. If you answered "no" to three or more, you should put some serious thought into whether you have the time or energy for a newborn.
1, 2, 3, 9, 10, 11, 13, 17, 18, 20, 22, 24, 25, 27

If you answered *yes* to the following questions, then you need to think long and hard about if you're ready and/or able to give up your free and easy zombie lifestyle. But if you answered "no" to these questions, then you're well on your way to making the sacrifices necessary to be a good parent.
5, 6, 7, 12, 21, 23, 26

If you answered *yes* to the following questions, then put down the OshKosh B'gosh catalog, because you are NOT ready to face the work and succulent temptation that comes with having a baby. However, if you answered emphatically "no," then you just might have what it takes to raise a happy, healthy zombie baby.
4, 8, 14, 15, 16, 19, 28

YOU WENT AND MADE A BABY ANYWAY

No going back now, you've gone ahead and infected an infant, making it yours as they slowly morph from human baby to crawling corpse in your loving home. Assuming you want the little ankle-biter (and weren't just too full to finish it after gorging on its breather parents), be sure to cover the baby basics.

Baby-proof your house. While the little monster won't be crawling around for a bit, it's a good idea to prepare early. Install plug protectors in the outlets, latches on the cabinets, and bars on the little one's windows.

Provided a safe crib for the little nipper. Securely attach chicken wire to the sides of your little one's crib. It may be small, but it is sneaky.

First Feedings. Have you decided on bottle-, or breast-feeding? Studies show the latter will lead to a more socially maladjusted child, but it requires nursemaids, lots and lots of nursemaids.

Toys. A bone left over from last Thanksgiving's turkey or a piece of car tire will help strengthen the baby's jaws and aid in the uncomfortable teething process.

Car Safety. While we recommend the standard carrier/car seat/ rear-facing combo, a sturdy cardboard box in the trunk will do the trick quite nicely. Wedge it securely between the spare and a fifty-pound bag of sand or sidewalk salt.

Germs. Your little devil is ripe with festering ickys. Don't let a lifer you aren't planning to eat hold your wee one unless they're properly protected by a welding mask and a pair of sturdy work gloves.

OK, YOU ATE YOUR BABY. NOW WHAT?

We warned you, didn't we? But you just couldn't resist the temptation, could you? So small and helpless as they slowly shed their humanity, they just scream, "Eat me!" Not many of the life-challenged are able to walk away from such easy pickings, and you were no different.

BREAKING THE BAD NEWS

Calm down and take a deep jagged, breath. Have you told your spouse? You may want to hide the truth as to why the little nightmare hasn't been clamoring underfoot. It's better you just bite the bullet and fess up.

Sit your partner down in their favorite shallow ditch to prep it for the news. Make it comfortable, offer it a snack or perhaps a pre-confession shoulder massage to ease away the day's tension before dropping the bye-bye-baby bomb.

DEALING WITH THE REACTION

Be ready for the various stages of mourning: unholy rage, then furious screaming, followed by anger with reflection, and then hopefully distress with understanding. This is going to be explosive no matter what, so brace yourself for the onslaught by putting on your running shoes before you talk. Consider preparing a safe room you can quickly lock yourself away in, or wildly brandishing a flamethrower to ward of an attack.

Let it vent its emotions without interruption from a safe distance. Remember that you don't want to discount its feelings, especially at such a painful time. Once the initial apocalyptic rage has subsided, it will likely be miffed that you didn't leave some leftovers for it. But what's done is regrettably done, and there's no going back at this point.

THE APOLOGY

You need to admit that you were wrong and make no attempt to justify your actions. It doesn't matter if all you really wanted was a taste. You should not have been "pretending" to nibble on those adorable toes when the little piggy was "wee wee weeing all the way home," so you have no right to be defensive. It doesn't matter that you're a flesh-eating creature; there are social mores that even you need to be adhere to. This time you truly crossed the line.

So now you must grovel. In words, in gifts, in favors, in chores, in all ways possible say, "I'm sorry." The penance for this is going to be big. Has your spouse been after you to repaint the slaughterhouse? You better come home with some paint samples. Has it been eyeing up a neighbor's fine china? Time to serve up that neighbor on their own silver platter.

FORGIVENESS

It's going to take some time and a lot of doing, but you can ulti-mately atone for this horrendous, unspeakable act of monstrous gluttony. Eventually you'll move on and will be able to put this embarrassing moment of weakness behind you and look at it as an unlife lesson in restraint.

Your partner will stop bringing up the baby every day in bouts of screaming, crying, and limb ripping, but once in a while it will probably take out a box of pictures and baby booties that will revive some old pangs and lead to more face ripping. If it truly loves you, then it will eventually forgive you. But it won't forget, because that was some pretty serious shit you did.

BEST WISHES!

This guide was written especially for you as a beacon in the foggy night of amour. With this wisdom, a lovelorn and romantically confused revenant can find their own path. My hope is that it helps you in your shuffling journey toward ever-eternal happiness with another.

Just as every scab is different, so too, is every zombie. You each have unique hopes, aspirations, and sleepless dreams of attaining a well-oiled relationship. While this book is no guarantee for the fulfillment of those longings, it can at the very least send you down the right corpse-strewn path.

I wish you many more days and nights of productive stalking, bellies engorged on still-warm flesh, and, most importantly, a post-soul mate to call your very own!

ABOUT THE AUTHOR

Jeff Busch graduated from Zombie High, class of 1964, and staggered on to receive a PhZ in zombieology. He is holed up in his family's reinforced bunker in rural Illinois. When not writing and illustrating, he spends his time patrolling the stronghold's perimeter, checking the deadfalls and snares for any undead that have breached the oil-filled moat and wandered onto the property.

He, his wife, and their three children are well-versed in all manner of weaponry, and are as comfortable firing a Heckler & Koch PSG-1 sniper rifle as they are wielding a Nepalese Gurkha knife.

Dr. Busch loves movies, long walks on the beach, and visits from friends. Just be sure to call ahead, since you probably don't know where the claymores are buried.

ACKNOWLEDGMENTS

Once again I'd like to thank my lovely, talented, and understanding wife, Michelle, who inexplicably allows her adult husband to hole up in his studio with his music and write about zombies.

I also would like to thank Katherine Furman, my wonderful and understanding editor at Sterling, who graciously walked me through a myriad of confusing and treacherous mazes in the creation of this book.

I'd like to thank Nathaniel Marunas for getting the ball rolling on this project and for adding his own unique talents.

I'd like to thank Dunkin' Donuts for the coffee that fueled many late nights, Internet radio that kept me entertained during those long nights, and finally, the many fans of *Zombie Universe* and the *Zombie High Yearbook '64* who were always there with kind words of praise and encouragement.